♡ For my sweetheart, ♡
This is for you Heather because I care, so please don't take this as an insult. You have an incredible body, this book isn't made to improve on perfection (Miss Universe).
I got you this book to make sure you are maintaining perfection properly, if you are, then congradulations? Read This for me, but also for yourself.
Thanks baby. I'm only looking out for your best interest, which, right now
IS ~~are~~ also mine!
Luv Your Steve-O ♡

THE NUTRITION CHALLENGE FOR WOMEN

THE NUTRITION CHALLENGE FOR WOMEN

LOUISE LAMBERT-LAGACÉ

Published in 1989 by
Stoddart Publishing Co. Limited
34 Lesmill Road
Toronto, Canada
M3B 2T6

First published in French by
Les Éditions de l'Homme
(Division de Sogides Ltée)

CANADIAN CATALOGUING IN PUBLICATION DATA

Lambert-Lagacé, Louise, 1941–
The nutrition challenge for women

Translation of: Le défi alimentaire de la femme.
ISBN 0-7737-2284-X

1. Women – Nutrition.   2. Women – Health and hygiene.   3. Cookery.
4. Menus.   I. Title.

RA784.L3513 1989   613.2'088042   C89-093439-8

Translation by
Helena Scheffer and Diane Norman

Printed in Canada

To
Pascale
Janique
Marie-Claire

Contents

Introduction: My Eating Odyssey   *1*

THE CHALLENGE

1   Women's Dietary Deficiencies   *9*

OVERCOMING THE OBSTACLES

2   Fear of Gaining Weight   *21*
3   Lack of Time   *40*
4   Eating Out   *60*
5   Living Alone   *72*
6   Unconventional Diets   *84*

SETTING NEW PRIORITIES

7   Less Fat!   *95*
8   More Iron!   *106*
9   More Calcium!   *118*
10   More Magnesium!   *130*

ON YOUR WAY!

11   Menus That Meet the Challenge   *143*

Appendix/Other Missing Nutrients   *154*
            Supplements
Bibliography   *172*
Index

THE NUTRITION CHALLENGE FOR WOMEN

Introduction:
My Eating Odyssey

Despite the countless recommendations of innumerable diet books—many of them best-sellers—women continue to lose their battle with fatty tissue. Nutrition books written for pregnant women deal primarily with the baby's immediate needs, often ignoring the mother's long-term health needs. The mass of data on calcium and the mature woman's needs concentrates on increasing daily intake while overlooking completely the dietary context of daily menus and lifestyles into which these extra milligrams must fit. And while there are marked differences between the nutritional needs of men and women, and it is acknowledged that modern women encounter considerable difficulties in meeting their nutritional needs, very few authors have really underlined the importance of these facts. Books that analyze these differences are rare indeed.

Many women today juggle roles inside and outside their homes but have no idea how to prevent chronic fatigue and complete exhaustion. They have increasingly overloaded schedules and devote more and more hours to a wealth of activities that do not include sitting down for a proper meal. More and more women have jeopardized their health and vitality by following radical fad diets which may be badly interpreted or even *wrong* for particular individuals. These women who need energy so desperately often weaken their resistance instead, as well as losing out on the pleasures of good food and healthy eating.

Women need nutritional information adapted to their cultural and contemporary lifestyles. They need to adjust their eating habits to their changing roles, to be guided on *how* to regain a state of adequate nutrition. But the available literature on nutrition does not serve them well.

The purpose of my book is to rectify this.

I have not always eaten well. . . .

As a small child, I adored pralines. These luscious home-made relatives of caramels were my own super-pleasure-food. Though I did not have them often, I used to dream of them, and had the opportunity arisen, I could have gorged on them. . . .

I was chubby in primary school. Spiteful little tongues called me "Fatty", difficult to accept even at that tender age. The pediatrician declared me allergic to dairy products. That would complicate my menu—and my life away from home, during summer vacations especially.

My bulges continued throughout adolescence, when I often spent hours in shops looking for *the* flattering straight skirt. I had no trousers in my wardrobe: they could not hide enough of me! The problem was my sweet tooth: if I took even a taste of rich goodies, I would always overindulge.

As a student dietitian, I dreamed of having the willpower to eat properly and so be slim like my classmates. The more I dreamed, the more I skipped meals, and then the more I would stuff myself with cookies and chocolate to compensate for frustrations and disappointments. I ate alone, without witnesses. The term "bulimia" was not used then, but after these food binges of mine, I experienced the dreadful mornings-after, followed by days of fasting and remorse. I came to regard the bathroom scale as my enemy!

The summer I was married, I did manage to lose a few pounds, but my eating habits had not really changed. A first pregnancy at twenty affected my health. Two more in short succession left me fragile, with my hands full . . . but I was slim! Though proud of my figure, I was neither well fed nor full of energy. I anxiously watched over the food of my three daughters, prepared meals for my husband and our friends, but more or less ignored my own needs. I was a good wife and mother— a typical woman!

My return to work in the field of nutrition at age thirty changed my outlook on foods and eating habits. I wrote articles on my subject for *Châtelaine* and, between 1973 and 1982, published books in which I pleaded the case for food without sugar, and meals without meat. At the time, this was a fairly radical swing, but I enjoyed the challenge of presenting convincing evidence. I became successful, too, and formed a higher opinion of myself. At last I could taste sweetness and not feel obliged to gorge; I could experience disappointment and not empty the cookie jar. Positive thoughts about myself, my performance, filled the gap that used to be filled by cookies! This sense of accomplishment took over the need to indulge in food.

At age forty-seven I think I have found the foods that suit me, that give me the energy to do what I want to do. I no longer fear the bathroom scale. I choose what I call "good investment" foods, favoring a semi-vegetarian regimen with small portions of fresh fish and poultry and a meal with fresh liver at least twice a month. I never count calories, but I avoid highly processed foods and those that have been fried, sugared, and salted. Today I am more attentive to the messages my body sends me, and I choose foods that are good to me.

I love eating, selecting recipes, planning menus, creating little dishes, going to the market with my husband, celebrating with beautiful foods and savoring sublime meals. . . . I don't spend hours in the kitchen every day, only on special occasions. I never skip a meal and nibble without a qualm; my body demands regular refueling. Food is an important part of my life, a pillar of my well-being!

My odyssey is hardly unique, but it has convinced me of the links that exist between self-esteem, better food habits, and good health.

MY CONCEPT OF HEALTH

My concept of health has also evolved over the years. Today, the definition that I accept has nothing much to do with "absence of disease." Rather, it is the ability to smile at life and to be vibrant, attuned, and open-minded, with no self-imposed limits. Good health is an attitude rather than a condition. I try to be healthy in my body, in my mind, and in my heart—in tune with the universe. At the same time, I realize that sustaining this attitude is a life's work.

Health cannot be negotiated in a practitioner's office—neither with traditional nor alternative therapies. Health is generated by our most positive thoughts and actions and permits us to function to the maximum of our potential. I proceed each day by looking at life on the bright side, by being attentive to what is going on within me, and by attempting to respond through my own resources. I may look to various practitioners for help, but I remain in charge of my lifestyle and of any improvements that I deem necessary.

At each stage of life our body sends us messages; these messages change and give us the chance to readjust our strategies. Good health is not a static condition, but one that demands continual readjustment.

Rosette Poletti, a Swiss nurse of international renown, shared her vision of health with us in Montreal in the fall of 1987. Paraphrasing her we could say: the more conscious women become of what is good or bad for them, the more they strive to discover their fundamental needs, the more balanced their interpersonal relationships become, the more significance they find in their lives — the healthier they will be.

This global concept of health appeals to me, even though it is so much broader than the convention of a nutritious meal. That meal remains fundamental, however. Good nutrition is an essential part of any attempt to grow and flourish, and to be healthy.

An undernourished woman, on a diet or bulimic, tired or constipated, plagued with physical discomfort that interferes with her daily living, cannot possibly be attentive to her inner needs or to her relationships with others. Such discomfort interferes with subtle messages that the body might be emitting. How can a woman set aside time for discussion, for exercise, for relaxation, or for reflection if she is hypoglycemic, anemic, obsessed by her weight, or stuck with digestive problems?

Women's health is necessarily related to proper nutrition, but it is essentially the result of happy, positive thoughts about life.

MY WORKING STRATEGY

This book has been germinating in my head for several years, fed and watered by my thoughts, my reading, and by my work. There were at least six different versions before it reached this final form.

I have examined scientific articles and attended conferences and seminars to learn all I could about the relation between nutrition and women's ailments and outright illnesses. For the last twelve years in my nutrition-counseling practice, thousands of women have shared with me their anguish about weight problems and their questions about food.

For the last five years, in collaboration with a doctor (Diane Corbeil) and a psychologist (Nicole Trudel), I have offered workshops on menopause. These sessions (sponsored by the University of Montreal) have deepened my appreciation of the nutritional problems facing women at the midpoint of their lives. Then, in the spring of 1986, lecture-discussions that I presented in several cities enabled me to examine the nutritional concerns of many hundreds of women, ranging in age from twenty to seventy-five.

Three dietitians, of whom two are mothers and one is a mother-to-be (Cynthia Dougherty, Sheila Dubois and Suzette Poliquin), have assisted in the development of this book. They have shared their experiences with me and commented on my own findings. As I proceeded with my book, I debated with myself. Should I use scientific language to convey the conclusions of well-founded research? Or should my tone be more personal, so as to share both my clinical experiences and my own feelings with my readers? Finally, I decided that I must combine the two!

At last I managed to say "no" to projects, to invitations, to telephone conversations. I had to create the space I needed in which to write this book while my life as a woman, a mother, a wife, and a dietitian still went on. It was quite a challenge, often very difficult, sometimes even intolerable!

THE BOOK'S GOAL

Let me say at once that this book is not meant to create new doubts or arouse guilt feelings in women who have been eating poorly for years. It is never too late to decide to eat better. Knowledge—in this case, knowledge about nutrition—is power to be exercised according to one's own pace and inclinations.

I begin my book by demonstrating for women their nutritional vulnerability, and showing just how great the gap is between the food needs of men and of women. I go on to try to shed new light on the reasons for women's dietary habits. I want to banish their obsession with thinness, redefine the chronic time shortage from which they suffer, address the inadequacies of restaurant menus, help them come to terms with their times of solitude. This book will also serve as an antidote to past and future radical diet restrictions.

My book is founded upon a nutritional strategy that is adapted to the needs of essentially healthy women, be they white-haired or adolescent, students or housewives, retired or at the peak of a career. Tables for the mineral and vitamin content of certain foods are included as an additional tool.

The only cautionary note I would offer is to women suffering from acne, arthritis, cancer, diabetes, excess cholesterol, hypertension, hypoglycemia, multiple sclerosis, or any other illness. While they can profit from the advice given in this book, they should also seek individual nutritional guidance for their specific needs.

Although this nutrition challenge does not pretend to give all the answers, it *does* offer a broader, more comprehensive view of practical dietetics specifically for women.

THE
CHALLENGE

1

Women's Dietary Deficiencies

Women are at a turning point in the history of their eating habits. Never before have women eaten so little, and never before has there been such a wide gap between what they eat and what they actually need.

Nutritional surveys conducted in Europe and in the United States during the last few years could not have come at a more opportune moment. They underline important deficiencies in the eating patterns of both active young women and older women, and reveal serious flaws in the menus of adolescents, sportswomen, and pregnant and nursing women. Every one of these studies confirms that the foods women eat leave them short of a whole group of nutrients that include at least four minerals and two vitamins. The surveys reveal a deplorable nutritional situation:

- One woman in five has *no* iron reserves.
- One woman in ten is actually anemic.
- Adolescents as well as active women eat only about half of the recommended calcium. Worse, calcium consumption tends to decrease as women get older, precisely when menopause brings an increased need for calcium.
- Many women do not eat sufficient foods that are rich in magnesium and in vitamin B_6.
- Many pregnant women do not eat enough to support a normal pregnancy and maintain their own vital nutrient reserves.
- Certain women lack protein, especially those who have opted for a meatless menu.

This disastrous balance sheet is topped off by the fact that a majority of women eat too much fat and not enough dietary fiber. Men, too, eat excess fat and too little fiber, but women seem to accumulate nutritional deficiencies. The young adolescent girl tends to have more nutritional deficiencies than a boy of the same age and this disadvantage will be maintained throughout a woman's lifespan. Numerous studies confirm this fact.

QUANTITIES HAVE BECOME INADEQUATE

Many modern women choose to eat very little, in order either to lose a few pounds or to stabilize their weight. And quite apart from those on diets, women in general eat less today than their mothers, who ate less than their grandmothers. . . .

Even though many women combine the roles of wife, mother, and wage earner, and expend more nervous energy than ever to cope with these multiple challenges, they use less and less physical energy to do their domestic tasks, to get from one place to another, and to adjust to external temperatures. This is because women's metabolism has gradually adapted to the automatic washer and dryer, the dishwasher, the automatic defrost refrigerator, the steam iron, the vacuum cleaner, the food processor, the word processor, the heated car, the air-conditioned office, the fur coat, the down quilt. . . . Women's bodies have noted these energy savings, and appetites have been reduced so that they can be satisfied by less and less food. This adaptation has taken place over several generations, without women even being conscious of it. As a change, it affects only *quantities* of food consumed.

There is a snag, however: as portions have diminished, the availability of less nourishing foods has increased—and this has not helped matters at all! Our grandmothers and great-grandmothers had never heard of potato chips or instant foods or dietetic foods or soft drinks. They regularly ate real potatoes, whole grains, and real bread.

Today's women have been more than exposed to the first generation of transformed, refined, and diminished foods. Over the years, women may have encouraged the first triumphs of food technology—permanently fresh white bread, completely hydrogenated fats, impoverished rices, and ultra-sweet fruit-flavored powders—but by so doing, they have reduced the vitamin and mineral content of their menus. Nor have women compensated for the shrinking portion size by choosing foods of better quality. Instead, they have eaten less and less both in quantity *and* in quality. Statistics derived from surveys of representative groups reveal that contemporary North American women on average consume only 1,500 to 1,600 calories a day. Most women do not manage to satisfy their vitamin and mineral needs on 1,500 calories a day. Even a ration of 2,000 calories seems inadequate if poor foods are chosen.

European researchers who have studied the types of food eaten by contemporary women have found that nutritional needs are not satisfied because one-third of the calories consumed come from foods of little nutritional value: soft drinks, wine, crackers, cookies, and the like. Women today, on average, eat 400 to 600 calories every day that bring them no nutritional benefit whatsoever, or very little.

The verdict? Today's women do not eat very much and since they do not eat enough nutritious foods, they can no longer meet their nutritional needs.

PROBLEMS WHICH DO NOT CONCERN MEN

Men have also adapted to reduced energy expenditure and they eat less than did their ancestors a century ago. But since men are usually taller, more muscular, and more physically active than women, they continue to eat more than women do. Surveys indicate that men absorb, on average, 700 to 1,000 more calories per day.

Men have other advantages. Their physiological needs are relatively stable throughout their adult lives, and are nutritionally less exacting. Men do not go through pregnancy or lactation or experience the hormonal swings of menstruation and the menopause. They do not need to adjust their menus to compensate for a monthly loss of iron; they never have to eat to assure fetal growth or milk production. They do not have to increase calcium intake because of a sudden loss of hormones at menopause. Adult men's iron needs are 40 per cent less than those of women of the same age.

Even if a husband's menu is exactly the same as that of his wife, he comes out the winner! A survey carried out on 1,800 couples living together and sharing the same meals confirmed the significant advantage retained by the husband. Because he averages 700 calories per day more than his wife simply by eating more of the same meals, he manages to get more calcium, more iron, more magnesium, more phosphorus, and more vitamins of the B complex. More food means greater nutritional security and a wider margin of safety. More vitamins and minerals are consumed when there is more food on a plate. Men are thus much less likely than women to suffer nutritional deficiencies.

The conclusion is obvious: men eat more than women even though they have less complex nutritional needs. The nutrition challenge for women is therefore infinitely more demanding.

A COMPLEX RELATIONSHIP WITH FOOD

From a strictly dietetic point of view, women's menus may fail to satisfy their nutritional needs but since women's interaction with food goes far beyond simple dietary considerations, we must look at many other aspects of this complex relationship.

Eating is not simply swallowing food! Eating involves every aspect of our being: physical, rational, spiritual, emotional. When a person chooses to eat poorly, rational decisions have been set aside. The individual who knows intellectually that it is better to eat fresh fruit for dessert, yet heads for the chocolate cake when under some emotional strain is one example. Then there is the woman who is so depressed that she completely loses her taste for food. And frustration can lead to the ingestion of mountains of extremely sweet or salty foods.

Every human being has some degree of emotional reactivity with food, but women are more vulnerable because of their tendency to bear responsibility for the emotional well-being of others. Women, attuned to the grief and disappointments of those around them, feel for others as well as for themselves. Moreover, women's relationship with food goes beyond personal or family obligations. Food is interwoven with social obligations and restrictions, complicating matters even more.

Since prehistoric times women have been responsible for food; sometimes growing and producing it, more often simply buying and preparing it. Women even have the physiological capacity to produce the primary sustenance of the human race: mother's milk.

Nine times out of ten, today's woman does the food shopping; four times out of five she prepares meals alone. Most of the time she thinks of others, trying to please and nourish them as best she can, often neglecting her own preferences and needs. She cooks to satisfy her companion, she cooks to please the children, she cooks her friends' preferred dishes. . . . When does she cook what *she* likes? In theory, women should have power over food; in practice, as they strive to please, women yield this power to others. It has been this way for generations.

While some men cook the occasional meal, it is a rare male bird indeed who cooks on a daily basis! Even though men now share food tasks much more than their fathers or grandfathers ever did, they are only rarely their household's food manager. Men can do the shopping if the list has been drawn up by somebody else; they can make the dinner if the whole set of instructions has been left for them! That's how it is, and cultural norms take a long time to change.

By the same token, a man who does not like to cook will not be the target of any derogatory remarks. A woman with the same aversion will often be criticized. Even her femininity may be questioned! A woman may hate to cook, but she may also have little choice. Then, by working emotionally and physically to nourish others, she may be left with neither the energy nor the desire to feed herself.

How many women dream of that "someone else" who would take care of the feeding? Who would feed "them", and who would feed "me"? How many women only really enjoy eating when someone else has prepared the meal?

GLORY AND CONFLICT IN THE KITCHEN

Society is lavish with its praise for culinary success. Good cooks revel in their moments of glory! Who hasn't seen a woman's competence judged by the height of her cakes, the texture of her puddings, and the subtlety of her sauces?

What about the woman who does not like to cook or whose cakes fall? Does she miss out on all the glory? Does she have any other way to win the admiration of her family and friends if she has no profession other than homemaker, or if her job outside the home is not rewarding?

How is it for men? A man's culinary efforts are praised, even if they fail, simply because they *are* a man's efforts. And his self-esteem is not likely anyway to depend on the praise, because he usually has other sources of gratification, at work or in other outside activities.

Differences between men's and women's relationships with food are even more profound. A woman lives in constant ambiguity: her culture gives her the entire responsibility for nourishment and judges her on the lightness of her cakes, at the same time rating her on a slender waist, slim legs, and flat stomach! Yet how can women hone their cooking skills and reap the attendant praise if they keep their distance from the refrigerator and food? And if women choose the glories of cooking, how can they remain svelte and receive all the respect they deserve? And if the result of time spent in the kitchen is a somewhat matronly figure, how can women resist the trap of the self-imposed strict diet?

Some women spend more than twelve hours a day in close proximity to their refrigerator. They handle food from morning till night: lunch boxes, breakfast, children's midday meal, family evening meal, late supper for the team member coming home late. . . . How can these women manage still to find pleasure in eating?

Working women spend more time away from the refrigerator, but they are not necessarily any further away from food and food responsibilities. How can one refuse the coffee-and-cookie break when it's the chance for social contact? Or the fat-laden fast-food lunch when the only alternative is for you, the working woman, to prepare your own nutritious lunch *after* all the other hundred and one jobs at home? How does one remain serene at the end of the day when everyone—from cat to kids—is hungry and in want of food and attention? And when at last one sinks to rest in front of the tube, how does one resist the urge to nibble along with everyone else?

Food has so many functions in a woman's life that it is sometimes difficult for her to remember that its primary function is to bring proper nourishment to the body. Food imposes on each woman a heavy responsibility; it adds time to her already overloaded schedule; it may serve only to satisfy others; it may only momentarily relieve her own tension. But such indulgence is inevitably immediately followed by remorse. She will get fat. Supreme punishment!

Women are living so many conflicts around food that their vision of healthy food habits has become more and more obscure. Many women just don't know any more. Every day brings its load of obligations and frustrations that put paid to rational food choices. Weight accumulates. Women fall into the diet trap. They lose a few kilos—temporarily. They also lose all pleasure in eating, and may lose out on the job of living as well.

This vicious cycle has ruined many women's relationship with food.

NEW LIFESTYLES

Women have more than meals to think about! One out of every two women has two jobs, and often three: spouse, mother, wage earner. Many women work forty hours per week outside the home, and fifty hours inside it. One out of two mothers on the job market has one or more children under six years of age.

Researchers who have studied the impact of multiple roles on women's health have concluded that "superwomen" are in better physical and mental health than their sisters who stay at home. Women who have many roles have more opportunities to be appreciated and more excuses to be less than perfect in *every* role. These "superwomen" have fewer qualms about delegating chores. Compared to women who are uniquely responsible for only one set of tasks, more "superwomen" enjoy good health.

Yet during this process of emancipation, women are adapting their bodies and minds to meet new challenges. They seem still to be going through a period of transition in which they adopt—consciously or unconsciously—certain male behavioral characteristics. It is as if certain styles of behavior were a necessary ingredient for meeting the new challenges. Unfortunately for their nutritional well-being, women have also done incredibly well at catching up to male levels of consumption of alcohol and tobacco!

A nationwide survey conducted by Health and Welfare in Canada at the end of the 1970s documented these new habits and showed that three out of four Canadian women drink alcohol before age eighteen. Eight per cent of Canadian women between twenty and thirty-four drink fourteen or more alcoholic beverages per week. In fact young women now drink as much as their male counterparts.

The same survey showed that more men participate in regular physical activity of at least three hours per week. Women working outside the home take part in more intense physical activity than do women at home.

As far as tobacco is concerned the survey revealed that women smokers today smoke as many cigarettes as did men in the 1950s. One out of five fourteen-year-old girls smokes every day, compared to one out of seven boys.

Since women have been so successful at emulating men's *bad* habits, this increase in smoking and drinking makes it harder than ever to meet female nutritional requirements.

FEMALE AILMENTS

A woman often experiences discomfort that is linked to her menstrual cycle, her emotions, her poor food habits, or her social and domestic responsibilities. She has problems of well-being which diminish the quality of her daily life but which have nothing to do with "real" illness. And she has real illnesses that are almost totally unknown in males. In fact, some illnesses seem the exclusive prerogative of women.

• Seventy to ninety per cent of women suffer some degree of distress in relation to menstruation, including abdominal distension, uncontrollable appetite, headache, irritability, heavy blood loss, and excruciating pain.
• Four times more women than men are miserable because of

their weight. Bulimia affects ten times more female than male university students.

- In the United States alone, 80,000 women between the ages of twelve and fifty suffer from anorexia nervosa; eight hundred die of it each year. There are no figures available for men.
- Seven times more women than men are anemic.
- Many more women than men are overweight or obese, and women form the majority of weight-loss clinic clients.
- Eight women out of ten are victims of discomfort due to menopause, ranging from hot flashes or chills to memory loss and extreme fatigue.
- One woman in five develops gallstones between the ages of fifty-five and sixty-five, compared to one man in twenty.
- In Western societies, six times more older women than men of the same age suffer from osteoporosis. In Canada, 250,000 women are afflicted with the disease. Approximately 12 per cent of all women with hip fractures will die of complications related to the fracture. At least 15 million Americans have some degree of osteoporosis; high-risk subjects are white postmenopausal women. A Mayo Clinic research team determined that about 150,000 hip fractures occur each year as a consequence of osteoporosis.

The nutritional status of women is responsible for many of these problems, but the connection is not always made. Although a woman may not enjoy optimal well-being, she does not always show signs of the deficiencies described in medical literature. She may lack a whole series of minerals and vitamins but will only attract medical attention when there is a diagnosis of anemia or osteoporosis.

The social context explains some of women's ailments. Statistics are overwhelming: women are the hardest hit by poverty; they are most often the sole support of single-parent families; after age sixty-five women often live alone and isolated.

In spite of this sad state of affairs, women remain the guardian angels of everyone else's health. They dole out first aid, they make the family medical appointments, they accompany children to the doctor and the dentist, they stay up all night to tend the sick, they cook the special meals for other people's diets, they use their own sick leave to care for others.

A UNIQUE FOOD CHALLENGE

The nutritional, emotional, and social overview in this chapter allows us to glimpse the magnitude and the complexity of the food challenge that women face. The principal elements of this overview, unique to modern women, can be summarized as follows:

- A small food intake, which does not provide enough minerals or vitamins. Diminished quantities with increasing age, precisely when needs increase.
- Proportionately greater and more demanding nutritional requirements than men.
- Food choices which are not satisfactory, and indulgences which only serve to calm emotional hunger.
- The role of cook, often unwelcome.
- A society in which opulent parties and fine cuisine are sources of prestige, overweight a source of humiliation.
- Alcohol and tobacco consumption at an all-time high.
- A far busier schedule than in the past.
- Family responsibilities as exacting as they have ever been.
- Female ailments that have not diminished in spite of increased medication.
- Poverty in single-parent households headed by women.
- Caring for the well-being of others, leaving little time for women to take care of themselves.

Women must face their own unique food challenge. They must not compare their food habits with those of men. Women's needs are different, and specific to women.

THE
OBSTACLES
TO OVERCOME

2

Fear of Gaining Weight

Thousands of women have explained to me the reasons why they find it so difficult to eat better. Among the very valid reasons they express—many of which support the points already made in Chapter One—five seem to be common to all women, young, old, pregnant, or in the throes of menopause. These reasons are the five major obstacles that block positive changes in women's food habits, because they are part and parcel of a woman's environment, and have rooted themselves in her mind and in her being.

Obstacle 1 : Fear of gaining weight
Obstacle 2 : Lack of time
Obstacle 3 : Eating out
Obstacle 4 : Being alone
Obstacle 5 : Unconventional diets

It seems to me essential that I confront all five roadblocks before proposing a new route toward better food habits for women. Obviously the size of the obstacle differs for each individual, since age and social context are variable. Most women will, however, be confronted with one or more of the obstacles at any point of their lives, to a greater or lesser degree. Each woman should concentrate on the blocks that seem particularly relevant to her now, and be especially attentive to the set of solutions that is proposed.

Women can proceed to better food habits only *after* they have managed to overcome the obstacles in their way.

Whenever I meet my friend Marie-Louise, she has just completed a vegetable juice cure or is ready to embark on another crash diet. I've known her for thirty years, and she must have gained at least fifteen kilos over the years—diet or no diet! When I dine alone in restaurants, I sometimes overhear conversations at the next table. It never fails: the conversation always turns to calories or pounds lost or gained in the previous twenty-four hours. . . . Whether I'm at a baseball game, a hockey game, a tennis match, or the symphony, diet talk fills the air between mouthfuls of buttered popcorn, gulps of soft drink and beer, or sips of cognac. And at my diet counseling office, I see women who have been battling their body's true weight since childhood. How many tragicomic stories have I heard, featuring outlawed fruit, banished bread, stolen meals, sugar cravings, energy loss, and worst of all, pounds regained. This must not go on!

Industrialized society has created an obsession about thinness. A single model of female beauty is extolled at every turn. From this, are we to assume that a woman's value is based on the circumference of her waist and hips? Or that all women were designed to weigh the same?

This same society has also developed a whole infrastructure to combat obesity. This thinness industry perpetuates the problem. Weight-loss clinics, diet books, liquid meals, spas, gyms, and diet foods do everything possible to convince women that they should be uniformly skinny. They do nothing to help women respect their own model of health and beauty.

Half of all Canadians consider themselves too fat, while a survey conducted in 1981 found that only one woman in five actually exceeded her desirable weight by any significant degree. A study done in the United States shows that sixty-five million Americans are officially "on a diet" and that one woman in two wishes to lose weight.

A QUESTION OF HEALTH

Today, women can no longer draw a distinction between the weight that is best for their own health and the weight society considers desirable. They react to just one message: lose weight at any price!

For years, the media has equated slender "beauty" with

health and a normal figure with being overweight. Tabloids and best-sellers claim that all women who are the same height should weigh about the same, whether they are athletic or sedentary, twenty or sixty years old. They rarely point out that right from birth, women have more fat tissue than men, and that this difference is not a disaster but rather a fact inherent in women's makeup to help them function better throughout their lives.

Studies even indicate that women who are overweight face fewer health risks than overweight men. According to an important Norwegian study, women accumulate less cholesterol and triglycerides in their blood than men, after an equivalent weight gain. Women usually carry extra fat around their hips, while men store excess fat around the waist. Women are pear-shaped; men are apple-shaped. The location of the excess fat has an effect on health, and research now indicates that overweight apple-shaped men are more likely to develop problems such as diabetes and hypertension than pear-shaped women who are similarly overweight. (However, an apple-shaped woman will have the same health problems as an apple-shaped man!) What seems unfair is that it is more difficult for a pear-shaped woman to trim her excess padding than it is for an apple-shaped man to lose his spare tire. The reason is that the fat stored around the hips serves a special purpose and a woman's body uses it only for emergencies, for example when special hormones are secreted during pregnancy and nursing. Under normal circumstances, this fat is very stable.

At different times during a woman's life, some excess fat can be beneficial. A woman who is well padded when her baby is conceived is less likely to have problems during pregnancy or to deliver prematurely than a thin woman.

Women who carry *some* fat in their fifties are less likely to suffer from osteoporosis than thin women, because fat tissue helps transform a certain amount of estrogen and in a manner of speaking, replaces the ovaries upon their retirement. This added estrogen helps women absorb calcium better and keeps their bones more solid. One study has even shown that fat women have fewer hot flashes during menopause than thin women, undoubtedly because of the same mechanism.

While the thinness industry continues to encourage fifty-year-old women to yearn for the scale-reading they had at age twenty, the statistics that serve as a basis for the famous *Met-*

ropolitan Tables (1983 edition) reveal that a North American woman gains on average nine kilos (20 pounds) between her 18th and 60th birthday, this in spite of having followed an impressive number of diets. Statistics show, too, that the weights associated with the lowest mortality rates for women in 1980 were six kilos (14 pounds) *more* than the weights indicated in the 1959 tables.

The term "ideal weight", coined when the first *Metropolitan Tables* were issued, created such confusion that it is no longer used. Canada's Department of National Health and Welfare and other organizations now use the term "healthy weight" to refer to several different weights which will not be detrimental to the health of women of the same height. For example, a woman 1 m 60 (5'3") can weigh 50, 55, 60, or 63 kilos (110, 120, 132 or 140 pounds) without putting her health at risk.

This new concept put forward by British scientists now makes it possible for health professionals to measure excess fat, not excess weight. Healthy weight has become an international measuring tool. It sets the facts straight about the relationship between body fat and the risk of disease. Women should now be less afraid of weight gain and accept the fact that healthy bodies come in variable shapes. A Rubens model can be perfectly acceptable. Weight becomes individualized, and women no longer have to compare themselves to a single acceptable standard.

Although this new approach does not deny the difference between healthy weight, overweight, and obesity, it emphasizes the prevention of real problems rather than imaginary ones. Healthy weight is also called Body Mass Index (BMI) or the Quetelet Index. The formula is as follows: Body Mass Index (BMI) is equal to your weight in kilos divided by your height in meters squared.

The table on page 25 makes these calculations easy. All you have to do is

1. Find your height in the left-hand column.
2. Find your weight at the top of the column.
3. Circle the point where they meet. That is your BMI.
4. Compare your BMI with the following information:
   - 20 to 25 corresponds to the "healthy weight".
   - 26 to 27 is an intermediate zone tending toward overweight.
   - More than 27 indicates obesity and an increased risk of disease.
   - Less than 20 enters the thin zone, and also corresponds to an increased risk of disease.

The Healthy Weight (BMI)

Height (Feet)	Meters	46	48	50	52	55	57	59	61	64	66	68	71	73	75	77	80	82	84	86	89	91
Weight (Kilos) → **Pounds**		100	105	110	115	120	125	130	135	140	145	150	155	160	165	170	175	180	185	190	195	200
4 ft 9 in	1.45	22	23	24	25	26	27	28	29	30	31	33	34	35	36	37	38	39	40	41	42	43
4 ft 10 in	1.47	21	22	23	24	25	26	27	28	29	31	32	33	34	35	36	37	38	39	40	41	42
4 ft 11 in	1.50	20	21	22	23	24	25	26	27	28	29	30	31	32	33	34	36	36	37	38	40	40
5 ft	1.52	20	21	22	23	24	25	26	27	28	28	30	31	32	33	33	35	35	36	37	39	39
5 ft 1 in	1.55	19	20	21	22	23	24	25	26	27	27	28	29	31	31	32	33	34	35	36	37	38
5 ft 2 in	1.58	18	19	20	21	22	23	24	25	26	27	28	28	30	30	31	33	33	34	35	36	36
5 ft 3 in	1.60	18	19	20	20	21	22	23	24	25	26	27	28	29	29	30	32	32	33	34	35	36
5 ft 4 in	1.63	18	18	19	20	21	21	22	23	24	25	26	27	28	28	29	31	31	32	34	33	34
5 ft 5 in	1.65		18	18	19	20	21	22	22	24	24	25	26	27	28	28	29	30	31	32	33	33
5 ft 6 in	1.68		17	18	19	19	20	21	22	23	23	24	25	26	27	27	28	29	30	30	32	32
5 ft 7 in	1.70		17	17	18	19	20	20	21	22	23	24	24	26	26	27	28	28	29	30	31	31
5 ft 8 in	1.73			17	18	18	19	20	20	21	22	23	24	24	25	26	27	27	28	29	30	30
5 ft 9 in	1.75				17	18	18	19	20	20	21	22	23	24	24	25	26	26	27	28	29	30
5 ft 10 in	1.78				17	17	18	19	19	20	20	21	22	23	23	24	25	25	26	27	27	29
5 ft 11 in	1.80					17	18	18	19	20	20	21	22	22	23	24	25	25	26	27	27	28
6 ft	1.83					16	17	18	18	19	20	20	21	22	22	23	24	25	25	26	27	27

- A woman who is 5'5" tall and who weighs 50 kilos (110 pounds) has an index of 18 and weighs less than her healthy weight.
- A woman who is 5'1" and weighs 59 kilos (130 pounds) has an index of 25 and is within the range of her healthy weight.
- A woman who is 5'6" and weighs 61 kilos (135 pounds) has an index of 23 and is within the range of her healthy weight.

Any active woman between the age of twenty and eighty can calculate her Body Mass Index (BMI). However, a growing teenager, a pregnant woman or a nursing mother, an athlete or a woman over the age of eighty cannot interpret these figures in the same way, since her body composition is different.

THE TEENAGER'S NIGHTMARE

Obsession with thinness does not wait until adulthood. It penetrates the minds of little girls even in elementary school, and becomes more and more prevalent by adolescence. Half of all teenage girls consider themselves too fat. Health studies reveal, however, that only ten per cent actually have a weight problem.

One adolescent in three is afraid of gaining weight and the majority of teenagers consider weight control a "priority"; indeed, many young girls start their first "diet" before the age of sixteen, at a time when they are still growing.

Teenagers and young women who spend six months of the year on a diet, one out of every two days half-starving themselves, weigh on the average five kilos (12 pounds) more at the end of the year than their peers who do not diet.

The age of puberty seems to partially explain weight differences in young girls. The earlier puberty starts (eleven and under), the greater the likelihood that the girl will be overweight; the later the onset of puberty (fourteen and over), the less likely the young girl is to be fat. This predisposition to weight gain among girls who reach puberty very young may explain some weight problems, but it is not a universal phenomenon.

Adolescent girls are not the only females who live with an obsession with thinness. It is just that during a period when she is particularly aware of body image, the teenager is bombarded by media messages that amplify the craze for thinness and a single image of beauty. She spends hours endeavoring to define her own image in these terms—a particularly unprofitable experience because the adolescent's is a fledgling, changing image in comparison to the perfected, finished model. Her frustration is compounded by the fact that rarely is her weight, height, or figure found satisfactory. A sad story as the emerging woman works hard to obtain the perfect body and ruins her health in the process.

Her obsession may even be nourished by her family, with their constant talk about weight, calories, and fear of fatness. When a teenager hears nothing but discussions about diets at every meal from earliest childhood, she can develop "calorie-phobia" and her already deplorable nutritional situation may worsen. A 1983 study published in the *New England Journal of Medicine* revealed that some young victims of this type of obsession had stopped growing. Brought up with the fear of gaining weight, they had unwittingly stopped their normal development until the family doctor discovered the source of the problem and reactivated the growth process by prescribing a proper diet.

The authors of a study conducted among 33,000 young people across Canada stress that in order to overcome this obsession with thinness, teenagers must learn to value themselves. There is a significant relationship between high self-esteem and a healthy life; physical activity seems to be one of the keys. A young girl who is involved in team sports or regular physical activity appreciates her body's strength and is more attentive to her dietary needs. She eats better, since she knows that proper diet will keep her in shape. In so doing, she distances herself from negative body images; she learns to appreciate herself, no matter how much she weighs.

THE RISKS OF UNDERNUTRITION

Scientific journals contain countless articles about women who do not eat enough, women who have decided to employ drastic measures to become thin, and women who neglect both the quantity and the quality of the food they eat. Some eat like birds; others survive between unhealthy fasting and binging. Many women combine intensive physical training with a very strict diet. Still others choose foods that are stripped of any nutritive value. All are damaging their health.

One per cent of women on diets become anorexic and turn their diet into a true concentration-camp menu. They become caught up in a vicious circle and adopt a strict diet for life. They develop such strict control over food that they are happy only when they finally lose all desire for it. Even when reduced to skin and bones, they still see themselves as too fat. These women range in age from fifteen to fifty and come from all social classes. Low food intake often leads to cessation of menstruation, dry skin, loss of muscle tone, and hair loss—not to mention extreme fatigue and headaches. They refuse to take vitamin supplements, fearing that this will stimulate their appetite and so they become incapable of eating enough food to survive. Many even die of anorexia: in the United States each year, eight hundred women literally die of self-imposed starvation.

Other women cultivate the idea of losing weight by eating less, but find they cannot do it. To hasten the process, they start skipping one or two meals a day and become nervous and aggressive. Feeling excessively hungry, they become weaker and weaker and finally gorge themselves on mountains of food. Then they slowly become bulimic, eating alone, secretly devouring an astronomical amount of food in record time, finally falling asleep, stuffed with calories and remorse. Several thousand women experience this problem, seesawing from fast to feast, using laxatives and diuretics or vomiting to accelerate the "weight loss" process. This process is repeated whenever these women feel frustrated or depressed.

Such abuse of laxatives and diuretics dehydrates the body and affects the heart and kidneys; repeated vomiting can damage the stomach, resulting in excess acidity that can even stain the teeth. Not to mention the negative feelings these women have about their behavior, and the sense of guilt which increases anxiety and decreases self-esteem. Women often experience their first attack of bulimia while following a strict diet. The vicious circle sets in and persists as long as their diet remains unbalanced and nothing is done to deal with the more profound causes of the disorder.

Other women merely wish they looked like Jane Fonda or Raquel Welch! The wish may be understandable but it leads some women to adopt practices which are far from healthy.

Combining hours of excessive exercise with a strict diet is not very wise. These women are simultaneously issuing two major challenges to their bodies, which can deplete their precious reserves. When a marathon runner or an athlete overtaxes her system, she can affect her hormonal system and disrupt her menstrual cycle. Some young athletes or dancers even accelerate bone loss before the age of twenty. If their physical training program is too strenuous and their diet too strict, it can disturb their menstrual cycle; this type of imbalance can lead to infertility.

In another area of research, a Swedish study sought to find a relationship between the quality of diet of thirteen hundred women and the incidence of heart disease. The researchers, without reaching any earth-shattering conclusions, pointed out that a possible link may exist between low food intake and such incidence. They even suggested that a relationship may exist between inadequate vitamin and mineral intake and the development of cardiovascular disease in women.

Women who are so preoccupied with thinness that they do not eat enough food have no idea of the damage they are doing to their bodies!

THE PREGNANT WOMAN'S DILEMMA

When I was pregnant with my daughters who are now twenty-six, twenty-four, and twenty-two, each visit to the obstetrician began with a weigh-in. When my weight gain exceeded one kilo, the visit seemed more like a negotiating session than anything else! The fashion at the time was not to look pregnant and to restrict weight gain to about eight kilos (18 pounds) during pregnancy. In my case, it also caused many complications. Many studies since then, however, have shown that such an approach is dangerous, both to the health of the mother and to the overall development of the baby.

Although the official scientific message has been corrected, practitioners' views have not necessarily changed. In 1974, the American College of Obstetricians and Gynecologists came out in favor of a minimum gain of 10 to 12 kilos (22 to 27 pounds) over the nine months, on the condition that the mother's weight was satisfactory at the onset of pregnancy. Surprisingly enough, the corrected message does not seem to have reached future mothers—or, more importantly—their doctors. In 1980, the National Natality Survey (NNS) conducted by the U.S. National Center for Health Statistics revealed that one woman in five was still advised not to gain more than 10 kilos during her pregnancy.

This communications problem harms the women who are the most vulnerable. A considerable number of thin women, smokers, teenagers, women over the age of thirty-five, and women living below the poverty line do not manage to eat enough food and will never reach their ideal weight. They have more complications during delivery; their babies are more likely to be premature and/or too small, and they are more likely to lose them at birth. Other problems can also be anticipated since babies weighing less than 2.2 kilos (five pounds) at birth are much more likely to have neurological or psychomotor disorders than babies weighing three kilos (seven pounds or more).

Why this hesitation about discussing proper diet and adequate weight gain when the relationship between the weight gained during pregnancy and the infant's birth weight has been so clearly established by experts? A study conducted in Chicago showed that mothers who gained more weight by eating properly were three times less likely to have small, frail babies than mothers who had not made the same dietary adjustments. The Montreal Diet Dispensary, which counsels about two thousand pregnant women each year, has proved time and time again that a proper diet, adapted to the needs of the mother, promotes adequate weight gain and decreases the risk of premature birth and underweight babies, even in the most unfavorable circumstances.

A mother who has a healthy weight (see page 25) at the beginning of her pregnancy has all the odds on her side if she gains a minimum of 10 kilos. A regular weight gain of about one kilo (two pounds) a month for the first four months and about 500 grams (one pound) per week thereafter is adequate. A gain of five kilos (12 pounds) at twenty weeks is an indicator used by health professionals to check the overall development of the pregnancy. A woman who is already thin should gain weight before her pregnancy or in its first few months to ensure normal fetal growth. An obese woman, on the other hand, should not try to lose weight during pregnancy; it might be harmful to her baby.

Despite these findings, which have been recognized world-wide, 40 per cent of women are reluctant to gain the recommended amount of weight, and refuse to eat enough for two. They are under the mistaken impression that the fetus takes what it needs for nourishment and that they need not worry about their own bodies. They are underestimating the demands of delivery and nursing—forgetting their own needs, and once again depleting their reserves and their resistance.

Since most pregnant women in North America function on a daily deficit of 200 to 500 calories compared to official recommendations, it is not surprising that they are deficient in protein, B complex vitamins, iron, calcium, and zinc, and so risk harming their babies.

The same attitude prevails after the baby's birth, when new mothers dream of regaining their pre-pregnant figure a few weeks after delivery. What an unrealistic and harmful delusion! A nursing mother who eats less than 2,000 calories per day (minimum) is courting disaster. She will be unable to produce enough milk and will end up exhausted, with a hungry baby on her hands.

Rapid weight loss after delivery is not healthy. Nature has a much slower plan in mind. A mother who weighs two to five kilos (five to twelve pounds) more after delivery than before pregnancy uses the calories stored in the curves of her hips to meet the demands of nursing. Even if she does eat more food than before being pregnant, she regains her figure as fast as a mother who does not nurse.

Gradual weight loss will usually occur without counting or cutting calories, within six months of the birth. A strict diet only weakens the mother at a time when she needs all of her energy for mothering and fulfilling all her other responsibilities.

THE WEIGHT CHALLENGE AT MENOPAUSE

The woman whose weight never varies within a lunar cycle is rare indeed! And rare is the woman who never has premenstrual food cravings. Most women experience ups and downs in their weight and appetite: no figment of their imagination!

Many women complain of water retention and bloating a week or so before their period. Many pre-menopausal women whose abdomens are quite flat until about two o'clock in the afternoon may have the experience of watching their waistlines swell before their eyes. So much so that they may even have to change into looser clothing for the afternoon!

Some attempts have been made to link these fluctuations with the lifelong role of female hormones. Such studies show that a woman's metabolism—her energy transformer, so to speak—does not always operate at the same rate. This varies throughout the menstrual cycle, with metabolic activity increasing after ovulation and during the second half of the cycle. Women are then able to eat more and burn more calories. In fact, women tend to eat more food in the two weeks prior to menstruation; this difference can be up to 500 calories per day but does not result in any long-term weight gain.

Food preferences also vary during this second half of the menstrual cycle. A recent survey conducted among 250 female prisoners revealed that 40 per cent of the women craved sugar and chocolate just before menstruation, regardless of whether or not they were taking birth control pills.

Female hormones (estrogen and progesterone) play an important role in this whole process, and the slightest fluctuation in these hormones during the cycle affects metabolism and appetite. When these two hormones are no longer in balance (particularly prior to menopause), abdominal swelling becomes more frequent and pronounced. This imbalance of female hormones also affects the thyroid gland, which slows down the metabolism. Women burn calories less effectively and gain weight more easily at this point in their lives, even if they are eating less than they did at age thirty. Many women note a gain of two to eight kilos (five to fifteen pounds) around the waist . . . even if their diet remains exactly the same.

Nor does a woman who chooses hormone therapy to counterbalance her reduced hormone production have any easier a time controlling her weight. This phenomenon has yet to be explained. On the other hand, weight gain seems to be the body's response to this major reorganization of the hormone system. As we saw before (page 23), excess weight may decrease the incidence of hot flashes and the risk of osteoporosis. This may be a menopausal bonus!

So, although it may be difficult for some, it is much healthier to accept this weight gain at mid-life than to diet. A strict diet will only upset the metabolism even more, contributing to calcium loss, often causing weight lost to be regained (sometimes even *extra* pounds), at worst prolonging the risk of inadequate nourishment.

DIETS DON'T WORK

In the United States between July 1977 and January 1978, fifty-eight people died suddenly after being on a 500-calorie-per-day liquid protein diet. Of these people, sixteen women and one man had complete medical records that indicated they had no other reason to die. This man and these women had been on the diet for two to eight months. They had been taking vitamin and mineral supplements and had started eating solid foods again. Twelve of these people were under regular medical supervision. (The remaining forty-two people had other medical problems in addition to being overweight.)

The same symptoms of arrhythmia or heart failure occur among both anorexic women and obese women on very strict diets. Prolonged food intake of less than 800 calories per day seems to affect the cardiac muscles and can lead to sudden death. While strict low-calorie diets are not always fatal, they certainly do not promote women's overall health. Doctor Van Itallie, a well-known researcher in the field of obesity at New York's Columbia University, reports that the most frequent symptoms among strict dieters are fatigue, nausea, diarrhea, constipation, dizziness, intolerance to cold, dry skin, hair loss, muscle cramps, loss of libido, euphoria, insomnia, anxiety, irritability, and depression. The outcome is not any rosier: most of the time, the weight lost is regained!

Diets which are less severe cause less distress, but they do not result in any more weight loss since 95 per cent of dieters are never able to maintain their new weight. Whenever they end a new diet, they also risk adding a few centimeters to their waistline. . . . Dr. Bronwell, of the University of Pennsylvania's Faculty of Medicine, explains the yo-yo weight phenomenon by way of his experiments with rats. When he redesigned the rats' meals by alternating high- and low-calorie diets, they gained and lost weight, but the rate of gain and loss varied with each new diet. With the first diet, the rats lost weight in 21 days and regained it after 46 days. With the second diet, the rats lost the same amount of weight in 46 days but had regained it all in just 14 days! Weight loss becomes that much more difficult with weight being regained much faster. Unfortunately, this yo-yo phenomenon is not restricted to rats. Humans share the same vulnerability.

The metabolism, our calorie transformer, adapts quite quickly to a reduction in calories. After just a few weeks, it becomes accustomed to burning fewer calories while keeping the body going at the same pace. This new pace will be maintained for a few months after the diet ends. For example, a woman who loses weight by eating 1,200 calories per day will get her body accustomed to functioning on those 1,200 calories. When she goes back to her regular 1,700-calorie menu, however, she will gradually regain the weight lost because her metabolism will not have resumed its pre-diet combustion rate.

The research is unanimous: any reduction in calories can slow down the speed of calorie transformation by up to 50 per cent, so that a return to a more liberal diet will inevitably be accompanied by weight gain. The greater the difference between the diet and the individual's regular menu, the faster the weight will be regained.

A GENTLER APPROACH

This obsession with thinness and the war against fat has gone on long enough! Women must call a truce, for the sake of their bodies and their minds!

The gentle approach I suggest makes health the priority and relegates the bathroom scale to the attic. It bans the term "diet", a scheme which offers only a temporary solution and ends as a disappointing experience. It cannot be improvised the night before buying a bathing suit or on the eve of a new fashion season, however. Its goal is long-term food reform and it often does result in permanent weight loss. The pursuit of a state of wellness is considerably more positive and less stressful than any attempt to lose weight.

The gentle approach does not foster any illusions. It takes into consideration a woman's age, weight history, permanent genetic background, and lifestyle. A forty-eight-year-old woman who has been heavy since adolescence, who has been on three diets a year for twenty years, cannot hope to lose 25 to 30 kilos (55 to 65 pounds). She can certainly slim down by improving her eating habits, but she will never reach the unrealistic weight of her dreams. A young woman with obese parents who has been overweight by nine to ten kilos (20 to 23 pounds) since puberty may have a chance to slim down if she has not already tried sixty-five different diets, if she moves out on her own, and if she adopts new eating habits. Each situation is different.

The gentle approach begins by developing a positive self-image.

- All women have qualities that can be stressed: healthy hair, sparkling eyes, an engaging smile, a fine chin, an infectious laugh, beautiful teeth, good nails, clear skin, graceful gestures, a special charm, shapely legs, and so on.
- All women have manual and social skills and human qualities which can be developed further: they may be sports-oriented, intellectual, artistic, community-minded, spiritual, accomplished seamstresses, excellent knitters, good singers, witty hostesses, superb cooks. . . .

By establishing a balance sheet of your personal assets, you will be in a position to estimate their value. This balance sheet shows your true wealth, which has nothing to do with your waist measurements! This should be followed by an honest negotiating session with yourself:

- Will I continue to react to social and family pressures? Do I have the desire and the willpower to undertake serious changes?
- Do I really want to improve my health or do I just want to lose five kilos (12 pounds) for the umpteenth time?
- Do I *really* want to change my food choices, my eating habits, my exercise program, some of my snacks?
- What are my current pleasure foods? What healthy foods could *become* pleasure foods?
- What would I be missing if I substituted others for my current pleasure foods?

Once your negotiations are complete and you have decided to begin this gentle change, you should also think in terms of increased physical activity. This will sustain your metabolism at the same rate, since the food changes will tend to decrease its pace. Choose a form of exercise that you enjoy, which fits into your schedule. Think about your obligations and what you like before enrolling in any type of activity. Start slowly; don't rush into anything. A ten- or fifteen-minute walk after each meal gives good results without disrupting your daily routine. If you can integrate exercise into your life and make it as natural as brushing your teeth, you'll be more at ease physically, benefit from added oxygenation, and finally set aside the search for the "perfect body". When it comes to food, the gentle approach suggests the gradual addition of foods which offer more vitamins, dietary fiber, and minerals. Over the weeks, you will acquire new habits at your own pace and shape new relationships with healthy foods. Without any frustration, you can drop foods that contain nothing but sugar, salt, and fat, and work toward improving the nutritive value of your menu month by month. For example:

- Eat fresh fruit for dessert more often. Start by choosing your favorite fruits, then let yourself be tempted by whatever looks good at the market.
- Take the time to eat at least three times a day and consider mealtime a special time of day.
- Choose whole-grain bread instead of crackers and cookies, which contain more fat and sugar.
- Forget to butter your bread every second meal to start with; then forget to put butter on the table. Everyone will be better off!
- Choose new snacks. Replace candy, cookies, and chips with nuts, unsalted seeds, and fresh fruit.
- In restaurants, systematically order vegetables or salad instead of french fries.
- Replace pâté, pressed meats, and cold cuts with fresh meat or fish (liver, chicken, veal, beef, pork, fish, seafood).
- Decrease meat portion size, but *never* leave out protein at any meal.
- Try new cooking methods (bake, steam with herbs, microwave) to decrease fat content without reducing flavor.
- Make light desserts by replacing some of the sugar with spices such as cinnamon, nutmeg, vanilla.
- Add a raw vegetable at the beginning of each meal to increase intake of dietary fiber and vitamins.

- Replace high-fat cheese with low-fat cheese (see pages 99 to 102).

This list is far from exhaustive, but it lets you make your own choices as you make new discoveries about foods and nutrition. Weight loss is secondary to the acquisition of these new pleasures. "Pleasure" is the key word here, because without it, there can be no lasting change!

Using the approach I have just described, you must be a winner! You begin a new lifestyle at your own pace, doing as much or as little as you can. Make the changes that suit you and score new victories whenever a change is integrated into your life. Develop a better relationship with food and with yourself. Forget personal weight—instead, give more weight to your personality!

PROS AND CONS OF "LIGHT" FOODS

At one time, so-called diet foods were relegated to one shelf in a remote aisle of the supermarket. These were foods for diabetics and people suffering from high cholesterol or hypertension. That situation has changed considerably. Diet products are now called "light", "lite", and "lean" and can be found throughout the supermarket, in virtually every food category. They are designed to reach millions of consumers and in 1986 alone, they represented 20 per cent of total food sales in the United States!

The revolution is far-reaching. A host of products are now sweetened without sugar, using sugar substitutes (aspartame, NutraSweet, Equal). Fat substitutes (Simplesse and Olestra) for frying and baked goods are also anticipated in the not-too-distant future. . . .

You must be careful, however. Not all products with the word "light" on the label are necessarily low in calories. Foods sweetened with aspartame will not always help you lose weight. Even cyclamates (Sucaryl, Sweet 10, Sugar Twin) and saccharine (Hermesetas, Sweet'n'Low), which preceded aspartame as ingredients in dietetic foods, did not provide the anticipated results. A study of 78,000 women aged fifty to sixty-nine to measure weight variations over a year showed that the 17,000 women who regularly used artificial sweeteners experienced greater and more rapid weight gain than the 61,000 who had never used these products.

An experiment conducted in England with ninety-five young adults showed that drinking water sweetened with aspartame (NutraSweet, Equal) made them feel more hungry and less full than water sweetened with glucose. This undoubtedly explains why many people feel like eating a large dessert or a package of cookies after drinking a diet soda. Dr. Blackburn of the Harvard Medical School has attempted to refute the British conclusions but neither his nor any other serious study has been able to show that regular use of sugar substitutes promotes long-term weight loss.

Since aspartame first arrived on the market in the early 1980s, it has also been suspected of causing behavior problems in individuals sensitive to phenylalanine, one of the product's two components. A number of consumers have registered complaints. A scientific analysis of the 231 complaints received by the U.S. Food and Drug Administration has revealed that:

- Three times more women than men have complained of some discomfort (women drink more diet drinks).
- The discomforts described are not necessarily related to aspartame consumption.
- In many individual cases, the problems are associated with moderate aspartame consumption (one diet drink per day) and disappear when aspartame is eliminated from the menu.
- Headaches, insomnia, fatigue, and dizziness are the symptoms reported most often.

In the summer of 1987, the American Diabetes Association took a stand on the sugar-substitute issue. It recommended moderate use at all times and pointed out that:

- Saccharine (Hermesetas, Sweet'n'Low) crosses the placenta. Pregnant women in particular should not abuse these products.
- Aspartame (Equal, NutraSweet) is still under investigation and the effects of regular long-term consumption are not yet known.

Taking these facts into consideration, I do not recommend the use of sugar substitutes as part of the gentle approach. Sugar substitutes merely maintain the sweet taste of foods and in no way contribute to improving the quality of a woman's diet.

But women who would like to reduce their consumption of fat, of sugar, and of calories need not despair! Many foods fit the bill, whether or not they are sold as "light" foods. Various processes are involved here, and they include:

- Use of fruit juice instead of sugar:
  Pears canned in their own juice;
  Pineapple canned in its own juice;
  Fruit cocktail canned in white grape juice.
- Reduction or elimination of sugar:
  Unsweetened applesauce;
  Unsweetened fruit purées;
  Double fruit jams.
- Use of water or broth instead of oil:
  Water-packed tuna;
  Some light salad dressings.
- Reduction of fat content by 50 per cent:
  Fat-reduced light butter or spreads;
  Light margarine.
- Use of low-fat products such as skim milk and part-skim cheese:
  Some light soups (Campbell's);
  Frozen dinners (Stouffer's *Lean Cuisine*, Hi-Liner *Light Tonight*, Swanson *Le Menu*, *Weight Watcher* meals).
- Skim-milk products themselves:
  Skim milk;
  Skim-milk yogurt;
  Skim-milk cheese.

Check the label—always the best and most reliable source of information. The list of ingredients reveals the presence or absence of sugar substitutes (NutraSweet, aspartame), the type of fat and additives used. Additional information about calories, protein, starch, sugar, and fat content will also help you evaluate the nutritive content of these products.

Regular consumption of good-quality light products can help reduce your fat and sugar intake considerably. It's up to you to choose the right products and use them properly.

3

Lack of Time

In the last century the poet W.H. Davies wrote, "What is this life if, full of care, We have no time to stand and stare . . ."

Women today seem to have no time. . . . No time to breathe, to daydream, or to sit and think. Time to eat doesn't even appear on their daily schedule. Lack of time has become one of the major obstacles to a balanced diet. Schedule overload has become the enemy of mealtime. The trend toward rush-hour cooking makes things even harder for women who not only have to find the time to eat but also the time to buy and cook the food. Having less time to cook is not a serious problem, but *not having enough time to eat* is alarming!

In this fast-paced century, the most vulnerable of all women is the married working woman with small children. She works more than eleven hours a day. Single women or women who have no small children work two hours less per day, but their lives are just as fragmented: divided between career, immediate family, extended family, community, and friends. Instead of reserving a few hours for themselves, they hesitate . . . then put it off indefinitely. How many women allow themselves to be devoured by others and by worthy causes, unable to say no? Is it really a question of time or is it a problem inherent in most women?

Work schedules *are* improving though, according to surveys conducted in the United States and Japan. Over the past decade a trend has been observed: the number of hours devoted strictly to paid work has decreased and the number of leisure hours has increased. Although working mothers with young children do not necessarily benefit from this lightening of the workload, women in general have more free time than before. Unfortunately, they are quick to fill up this free time, to the extent that many feel as if they are living on a treadmill! One might ask why leisure activities have acquired the importance formerly attributed to meals.

I once treated a young woman with arthritis who, before coming to see me, had undergone a series of very expensive treatments. When we discussed how to improve her diet, she admitted that she had no time to eat. She gobbled her breakfast in the subway and often skipped lunch. Rearranging her schedule as a starting point was going to be even more important than changing her food choices!

Many women are living under tremendous pressure. Unfortunately, they seem to have lost their appreciation for mealtime and although they may enjoy dinner parties or special celebrations, they consider ordinary weekday meals a waste of time! They won't even sit down to eat, often gulping down fast snacks between two activities. Like many men, they underestimate the value of mealtime as nourishment for the spirit, a source of pleasure—in fact a high point of the day, boosting mental energy in a way that can't be calculated in terms of calories.

This time-crunch dilemma reminds me of a comment that a psychologist friend made when I mentioned that I had no time for a certain activity: "You can always find time to do what you want to do." Since then I never say, "I don't have time," but rather "I haven't taken the time. . .". I have become aware of the power I have over time. It's limited of course, but it allows me to say yes or no, to choose between what is important and what is urgent as the days and weeks go by.

AN EXCUSE, PERHAPS?

"Lack of time" is often a cover—an excuse for other reasons that are more difficult to admit. Let me introduce a few women, each of whom has thousands of clones in today's world and none of whom seems to have any time to eat. I'll play devil's advocate and suggest the real reasons behind this so-called lack of time. Then I'll propose some solutions.

CHERYL

Cheryl, a student, is nineteen. This is a very difficult year of school for her. She has trouble getting out of bed in the morning and is so late that she usually races out of the house without breakfast. At noon, she snacks on whatever she can find in the vending machines. At the end of the afternoon, she goes home, returning to school for 7 p.m. class. Of course she has no time for a sit-down dinner! After her class, she makes another trip to the vending machines. . . .

Cheryl's health problems

Cheryl has no resistance. She suffers from chronic flu and never really feels energetic.

The real reasons

Cheryl wants to be like everyone else and eat in the way they do. She hates to eat alone and is under the false impression that by snacking, she is taking fewer calories.

What should she do?

Cheryl could whip up an instant-breakfast drink in the blender or eat a yogurt before leaving the house in the morning. She could choose the best foods available in the vending machines. She could also heat up a frozen dinner in the microwave before leaving for her 7 p.m. class.

SUSAN

Susan, aged twenty-seven, is a young lawyer just starting her career. Her days begin very early and she often works past midnight. She doesn't really have time to eat at noon. She has a bit to eat at 6 p.m. between phone calls before leaving for her community group meetings. By the time she gets home, she's starving, and binges on anything she can find.

Susan's health problems

Susan is gaining weight and feeling less energetic. She has trouble concentrating, especially in the afternoon.

The real reasons

Susan would like to lose a few pounds and thinks she's found the way: skipping meals. Her strategy is backfiring, however, because her midnight raids on the fridge cancel out all her attempts at losing weight.

What should she do?

If Susan canceled a few calls and planned a half-hour break at noon and again at suppertime to eat a real meal or even a wholesome snack, this would give her a second wind. These short breaks would not be detrimental to her practice and also would save her from the desperate late-night eating excesses.

JANET

Janet is thirty-five. Every morning she prepares a good breakfast for Martin, aged three and Natalie, aged five, but she doesn't have a minute to spare to eat her own breakfast before driving them to the daycare center. She is a reporter, running from one interview to another from 9 a.m. to 1 p.m. She has to finish her articles by 4:30, then rush to pick up the kids before the daycare center closes. Eating at noon is out of the question, except for a sandwich in the car between interviews. By evening, she's totally worn out and feels as if she hasn't eaten for twenty-four hours.

Janet's health problems

Janet feels close to burn-out. Writing an article seems like an insurmountable task. She has no more patience with the children.

The real reasons

Janet takes care of everyone but herself. She's trying to be a superwoman but nearing the end of her rope.

What should she do?

The solution is simple: whip up some instant breakfast which takes just a few minutes to prepare and eat. Janet should take a lunch break before writing: soup or salad, a roll, cheese or yogurt. She could even eat in the office. The fifteen minutes it takes to eat will not seriously disrupt her schedule.

MARY

Mary, aged forty-three, is a successful businesswoman. She leaves the house every weekday at about 7:45 a.m. after a breakfast of toast, jam and coffee. She has at least six important meetings during the day and manages to attend a fitness class at noon. She finds no time to eat before 7 p.m. when she arrives home, exhausted and starving. Two or three times a week she is invited out. Dinner is never served until 9 p.m. and by then she is so tired she doesn't feel like eating.

Mary's health problems

Mary's last blood count showed excess cholesterol and deficient iron. Each working week, she can barely keep herself going until the weekend.

The real reasons

Mary is watching her weight. She wants to weigh the same as she did in her twenties, and hates eating alone.

What should she do?

Instead of toast for breakfast, she could eat a bowl of whole-grain cereal which provides more nourishment without adding extra calories or extra time. Mary could also eat a light lunch after her fitness class to keep her going for the rest of the day. If she added a quick pick-me-up (water and brewer's yeast) before leaving the office, it would be much easier to wait for a late dinner. Who knows—Mary might even be the life of the party!

ANNE

Anne is sixty. She has lived alone for the past five years. She has never held a paid job but is always willing to help worthy neighborhood causes. She leaves the house at about 11 a.m. and doesn't have time to eat lunch because it would conflict with her volunteer work. She returns home at about 4 p.m., helps herself to a few cookies and a cup of tea, then eats a light supper in front of the television.

Anne's health problems

Anne is tired from morning till night. Every joint hurts, but she has no identifiable illness.

The real reasons

Anne is lonely, especially at mealtime. She hates eating alone.

What should she do?

Anne should rethink her schedule and plan her volunteer activities to harmonize with her mealtimes. Then she could invite over a co-worker and they could eat together (see pages 72 and 75). Her diet would improve considerably and she would not be taking any time off her volunteer schedule.

Lack of time has become a convenient and socially acceptable excuse. But it *is* an excuse and it is important never to lose sight of the real reasons behind any excuse!

FAST FOOD OR INSTANT EATING

Did you know that a new McDonald's restaurant opens every seventeen hours? The fast-food industry has changed North American food habits and has drawn criticisms from nutritionists everywhere. Fast food is generally heavy on fat, sugar, and salt and deficient in dietary fiber. And what many people may not realize is that it has ruined the concept of a real meal.

Food that is quick to eat, gobbled down in three minutes on an uncomfortable bench, cannot be called a meal. A much better idea of a meal is food that's *quick to cook*, but is served at the table on a real plate with real utensils and is eaten at a reasonable pace!

I certainly empathize with women who want to spend less time in the kitchen and take advantage of all possible cooking shortcuts. But as much as I favor the idea of food that is quick to prepare, I deplore "fast eating" which has led to the decline of the real meal.

It's not the time you spend at the stove that nourishes, but rather the time you take to enjoy each mouthful!

STRATEGY THAT GIVES YOU TIME

What woman has not dreamed of eating well without spending hours in the kitchen? Here is a six-point strategy that will cut down on preparation time, provide you with balanced and nutritionally sound meals, and increase the amount of time you can spend at the table.

1. Choose Healthy Fast Foods

Good fast foods have not been too badly treated by the food industry. While not necessarily natural or organic, they do come to the rescue at critical moments, still containing very acceptable levels of vitamins, minerals, fiber, and proteins. They do not contain much sugar, salt, or added fat, and little or no additives. They can be divided into three categories:

Category A = High-protein foods
Category B = Fruits and vegetables
Category C = Grain products

Each category includes foods that are *ready to eat** and require no preparation. Others can be prepared in *ten minutes or less* (10) (from refrigerator to table).

Category A: High-Protein Foods

* Ready-to-eat cooked chicken (purchased)
* Cooked shrimp, fresh or canned
* Canned tuna or salmon
* Peanut butter
* Cheese (see list on pages 99 to 100)
* Yogurt and milk (skim, part skim or whole)
* Canned legumes (chickpeas, kidney beans)
(10) Boneless skinless chicken breasts, steamed (recipe p. 58)
(10) Fresh fish fillets or steaks (recipe p. 57)
(10) Lean ground beef
(10) Thinly sliced liver (recipe p. 111)
(10) Eggs: poached, scrambled, boiled

Some of the new "light" frozen dinners on the market can also be prepared in *twenty minutes or less (20)* from freezer to table. A 1986 analysis of 93 of these products showed that many contain a considerable amount of protein, little fat or salt, and few additives. Highly rated dinners are: McCain's *Lite Delite*; Stouffer's *Lean Cuisine*; *Weight Watcher* dinners; *Le Menu* by Swanson; High Liner's *Light Tonight*.

Although these meals are expensive, their cost compares favorably to similar restaurant meals.

Category B: Fruits and Vegetables

* Fresh fruit; wash and eat as is.
* Small jars of unsweetened puréed fruit; serve as dessert or pour over plain yogurt or ice cream.

* Unsweetened applesauce; sprinkle with cinnamon.
* A mixture of dried fruit and nuts; a good dessert after a light meal.
* Cherry tomatoes; wash and eat.
(10) Frozen unsweetened fruit; thaw in the microwave; serve as is or purée (recipe p. 56).
(10) Greens: lettuce, chicory, lamb's lettuce; sprinkle with vinaigrette.
(10) Fresh carrots; peel, cut into sticks and eat raw.
(10) Red, green, or yellow peppers; cut into strips or rings; eat raw.
(10) Cauliflower or broccoli: wash and cut into florets; serve with dip.

Category C: Grain Products

* Whole-grain bread with no additives
* Whole-wheat pita bread
* Ready-to-eat cereal (Shredded Wheat, muesli, bran flakes)
* Wheat germ: sprinkle over yogurt or cooked fruit
(10) Whole-wheat pasta
(10) Bulghur

Category D: Good Extras

(Add to meals or eat as a snack)
* Unsalted nuts
* Unsalted sunflower seeds

On evenings when you have a parents' meeting, concert, or class, when every second counts, use ready-to-eat foods*. Choose one (*) food from category A, one from Category C, and two from category B.

A. Protein	(*) cooked chicken
C. Grain Products	(*) whole-wheat bread
B. Fruits-Vegetables	(*) cherry tomatoes
B. Fruits-Vegetables	(*) applesauce and cinnamon

On evenings when you have a little more time, use some of the foods that can be cooked in ten minutes or less. Choose one (10) from Category A, one from Category C, and two from Category B.

A. Protein	(10) steamed fish fillet
C. Grain Products	(10) bulghur with parsley
B. Fruits-Vegetables	(10) broccoli salad
B. Fruits-Vegetables	(*) fresh strawberries.

Both suggestions will give you a balanced meal.

2. Shop at the Right Time

Who hasn't endured the torment of doing the grocery shopping at 5 p.m. on Friday or 11 a.m. Saturday morning when there are no more shopping carts, long lineups at the fish and meat counters, traffic in the aisles, and long lines at the checkout. What a waste of time!

You can save a whole hour of lineups and aggravation by doing your food shopping either early in the morning or at about 6 p.m. on Thursday or Friday.

3. Delegate Some of the Preparation

A young woman who was exhausted from working and commuting once came to see me about balancing her diet. After a few months of adjustments, she found her own solution. A friend of hers did not work outside the home and loved to cook, so she hired her as her caterer! This was their agreement: my client supplied her best recipes, paid for the food, picked up her frozen meals once a week, and also brought her friend gifts every so often.

Another woman, a working mother, asked her young afternoon sitter to do some of the food preparation. The babysitter cooked a few easy recipes once or twice a week, and each weekday would wash and peel the vegetables and make the fruit salad for the family's dinner.

One lucky mother received a special birthday gift from her twelve-year-old daughter: a commitment to cook one meal a week! The young cook had only two conditions: carte blanche when it came to the menu and a full fridge on her day to cook. What an exceptional gift idea! Perhaps it will inspire other children, husbands, friends. . . .

One of my friends hires a student for about five hours a week. The student does the shopping and prepares three or four good main dishes which can be frozen. My friend uses the meals as she needs them.

There are as many good ideas out there as there are smart women!

4. Encourage Participation

Why should women have to do everything? Why should they not be permitted to ask for collaboration concerning food-related activities and at mealtimes? A team takes less time and also provides excellent moral support. Children, friends, and spouses, please note all cries for help!

Doing the shopping together can be real pleasure. On Saturday mornings, when I leave home with my husband and my list, I feel as if we're going out on a date! I love discussing with him which foods to choose, and sharing delight in new discoveries. I even like carrying packages together!

Last-minute help can also save time. At breakfast, someone can set the table or prepare the fruit while someone else gets out the cereal and makes the coffee. At suppertime, a child or another adult can make the salad and the dressing. When it's time to do the dishes, many hands make light work—even to load a dishwasher!

The possibilities for cooperation are limitless—setting the table, slicing bread, grating vegetables, cutting fruit. The important thing is to *ask for help!*

5. Stock up on Fresh Produce in the Summer

Summer is the ideal time to stock up for the busy winter months. When things start to hum again in the fall, these supplies can cut cooking time down from an hour to less than twenty minutes.

Not long ago, it was commonplace to freeze uncooked fruit and vegetables, filling freezer bags with strawberries, tomatoes, leeks, red peppers, and the like to be used in soups and sauces. However, there are also advantages to cooking large quantities of soups and sauces when fruit and vegetables are at their peak. If you freeze strawberry coulis, asparagus soup, ratatouille, tomato sauce, peperonata sauce, or pesto in meal-size portions, you'll save hours of cooking time in the winter. When I come home from work, I often defrost the soup or sauce in the microwave, then serve the soup or pour the sauce over fresh pasta or cooked legumes and we're ready to eat!

Stocking up for winter can also be done in a team. I know some women who get together in groups of two or three to make sauces and pickles. One does the buying, another supplies the jars and freezer bags, while the other provides her kitchen. Then they meet to cut up the fruit and vegetables. Nothing prevents them from gossiping while they cook! When the cooking is over, they share the fruits of their labor. Not only do they save time, they also have a lot of fun!

To flavor winter meals, don't forget to stock up on fresh herbs (thyme, rosemary, savory, oregano, mint). Here's how. Tie together bunches of herbs at the stem, cover with a twist of brown paper or a paper bag, and hang to dry upside down from hooks in the ceiling or window ledge. That's how I keep my herbs. I cut off only what I need for my recipe. This method retains the flavor much better than storing herbs in glass bottles.

Make lots of pesto with fresh basil. This tasty Italian sauce turns an ordinary dish into something delightfully aromatic and special.

PESTO

Preparation time: 10 minutes
Makes about 8 cubes

1 bunch (2 cups) fresh basil, washed, dried, and firmly packed
125 mL (1/2 cup) virgin olive oil
3 cloves garlic

In blender or food processor, combine all ingredients. Blend until smooth. Pour into ice-cube containers and freeze. When frozen, empty into a plastic bag and seal.

One cube will boost the flavor of a soup or sauce for 4 people. Add a cube to tomato sauce, spaghetti sauce, rice pilaf, a dish of legumes or of tofu. Serve warm with your favorite pasta for a classic *pasta al pesto*.

6. Simplify Your Meals

There is always a complicated and a simple way to do everything. I automatically choose the simple method, which is often the healthiest! I use my food processor, blender, and microwave oven every day. In fact, I would have a hard time cooking without them! Here are some of my favorite short-cuts.

HEALTHY BLENDER BREAKFAST

Preparation time: less than 2 minutes
Makes 1 serving

1 fresh fruit (banana, pear, peach, cut into chunks) or
75 g (1/2 cup) fresh strawberries or other berries
175 to 200 g (3/4 to 1 cup) plain yogurt
2 tbsp frozen orange juice concentrate
1 tbsp wheat germ

Mix all ingredients in a bowl and eat as is, or pour into blender or food processor. Process until smooth and pour into a tall glass.

You can also add any of the following:

1 tbsp natural wheat bran
1 tbsp torula yeast
2 tbsp whole or chopped nuts or seeds

MINUTE SOUP

Preparation time: less than 10 minutes
Makes 2 servings

1 large carrot
1 onion
A few lettuce leaves

Cut the carrot into large chunks, quarter the onion, and tear up a few lettuce leaves.

Drop the vegetables into 2 cups vegetable or chicken stock and simmer for about 10 minutes. Then pour into the blender. Purée to desired consistency. When the soup is ready, add some herbs, seasonings, and a little oil or butter.

If you like, you can make a larger quantity of this soup and freeze it.

VITAMIN-RICH SNACKS

Preparation time: less than 2 minutes
Choose any of these or a combination.

Carrot sticks
Pepper strips
Cherry tomatoes
Fresh snow peas
Turnip sticks
Broccoli florets

HEALTH SALAD

Preparation time: less than 5 minutes
Serves 4 to 6

One Boston or romaine lettuce
Spinach leaves
Chicory or lamb's lettuce

Wash and dry the Boston or romaine lettuce and a few spinach leaves. Add some chicory or lamb's lettuce if available. Drizzle with vinaigrette just before serving.

VINAIGRETTE

Preparation time: less than 2 minutes
This quantity will lightly dress the Health Salad.

1 tsp Dijon mustard
1 tbsp wine vinegar
3 tbsp olive oil or other cold-pressed oil
Salt, pepper

Mix Dijon mustard with the wine vinegar, then add oil. The ratio of oil to vinegar should be 3 to 1.

VEGETABLES AL DENTE

Preparation time: less than 10 minutes (cooking time depends on the vegetable)
Quantity as required

Broccoli
Cauliflower
Carrots
Zucchini
Snow peas

Steam or microwave the vegetables, respecting their cooking times. Cut into small pieces to reduce cooking time.

LIGHT QUICHE

Preparation time: faster than a regular quiche, because there's no crust.
Serves 4 to 6

2 eggs, well beaten
500 mL (2 cups) 2% milk
4 oz (1 cup) grated cheese (mozzarella, partly skimmed, or similar)
1 cup vegetables, cooked and chopped (try a combination of leftover carrots, broccoli and peas)

Combine eggs, milk, cheese, and vegetables. Pour directly into a well-greased 8" Pyrex pie plate. Bake at 350°F for about 30 minutes. Cut and serve.

SEAFOOD SAUCE

Preparation time: less than 2 minutes
Serve with grilled or poached salmon steak or steamed shrimp.
Serves 2 to 4

125 g (1/2 cup) plain yogurt
2 tsp Dijon mustard
Salt and herbs to taste (try thyme or tarragon)

Combine yogurt, mustard, salt, and herbs and serve with warm fish.

GINGER SAUCE FOR WHITE FISH

Preparation time: less than 2 minutes
Delicious with broiled or baked halibut steaks.
Serves 2 to 4

2 tbsp fresh ginger, finely grated
25 g (2 tbsp) softened butter

Combine and spread over each steak immediately after cooking.

SUMMER SAUCE

Preparation time: less than 2 minutes
Wonderful with white fish like sole or cod
Makes 2 to 4 servings (can also be used as a dip)

125 g (1/2 cup) plain yogurt
35 g (1/3 cup) grated cucumber
1 green onion, minced
Salt and pepper to taste

Combine and serve over fish.

LIGHT SAUCE FOR POULTRY

Preparation time: less than 2 minutes
Very good with steamed chicken breast
Makes 2 to 4 servings (can also be used as a dip)

125 g (1/2 cup) plain yogurt
15 g (1/4 cup) parsley, finely chopped
20 g (1/4 cup) chives or green onion, minced
1 tsp cold-pressed oil
Salt and pepper to taste

Combine and serve over steamed, broiled, or baked chicken.

INSTANT DESSERT

Preparation time: less than 5 minutes
Quantity as required
Seasonal fruit makes the best instant dessert

1 quarter cantaloupe or
1 bowl fresh strawberries or raspberries or
1 pear or peach or
A few clementines or mandarin oranges or
1 bunch seedless grapes or
A few fresh figs

To win over those with a sweet tooth and to make the fruit more attractive, you can dress it up with fruit coulis (below), vanilla yogurt, a handful of toasted chopped almonds, or a spoonful of toasted coconut.

STRAWBERRY COULIS (SAUCE)

Preparation time: less than 3 minutes
Makes 250 mL (1 cup) coulis

160 g (1 cup) fresh or frozen unsweetened strawberries, thawed
1 tbsp lemon juice
1 tbsp or less liquid honey or maple syrup

Combine all ingredients in blender or food processor.

Taste before adding honey; adjust sweetness to taste. Pour a generous spoonful of sauce over fruit (or plain yogurt, for a healthy sundae). Garnish with a mint leaf.

Coulis can also be made with raspberries, peaches, or pears.

MEALS IN A MINUTE

You can prepare a complete meal for one or two in a steamer in a matter of minutes. Adjust quantities to suit your appetite. The next two pages contain suggestions for two complete meals that can be prepared in less than 20 minutes.

COMPLETE MEAL FOR TWO FEATURING HERB-STEAMED FISH

Preparation time: less than 15 minutes

Ingredients for the Meal
1 fresh salmon steak, about 4 cm (1 1/2") thick
Salt and thyme
3 medium carrots
1 small zucchini or 4 fresh asparagus spears
Seafood Sauce (p. 55)
Accompaniment: slices of whole-wheat bread

Dessert: 2 oranges
Toasted almonds

Pour 5 cm (2") water into the bottom of a pot large enough to hold an open steamer. Add a good pinch of salt and thyme. Cover and heat over medium heat.

Oil steamer to keep fish from sticking and put in salmon steak. Peel the carrots and cut into 10 cm (3") julienne strips. Wash zucchini (don't peel) and cut into sticks to match the carrots, or wash the asparagus and cut into 10 cm (3") pieces. Place the vegetables on the other side of the steamer.

When the water comes to a boil, place the steamer in the pot, cover, and steam for 7 to 10 minutes; after 7 minutes, check salmon with a fork to see if the fish is pink all the way through; if it is, remove from heat. If not, cook until pink. Prepare Seafood Sauce (p. 55).

Peel the two oranges, slice thinly, and place in two dessert bowls; sprinkle with toasted almonds. Put aside.

Divide the fish steak in two. Serve with the vegetables. Pour some sauce on the plate beside the fish. Don't forget the whole-wheat bread to complete the meal. Or the oranges for dessert!

Use the same recipe for fish fillets, but adjust the cooking time. Begin by cooking the vegetables and add the fish when the vegetables are nearly done. Serve with Summer Sauce (p. 55).

COMPLETE MEAL FOR TWO FEATURING CHICKEN WITH JULIENNED VEGETABLES

*Preparation time: less than 15 minutes
2 servings

Ingredients for the Meal
1 whole skinless boneless chicken breast
1 shallot (not green onion)
Thyme and savory
2 carrots
1 small package fresh snow peas (about 24 pods)
90 g (1/2 cup) bulghur (cracked wheat)
Fresh parsley, minced
Light Sauce for Poultry (p. 56)

Dessert: 2 fresh pears
1 baby-food jar puréed pears

Pour some water into a pot large enough to hold an open steamer. Crush shallot and add to the water. Add a pinch of thyme and savory. Cover and bring to a boil over medium heat.

In a smaller pot, pour 250 mL (1 cup) vegetable stock or water; bring to a boil and add the bulghur. Cover, reduce heat and simmer for 10 to 12 minutes.

Lightly oil the steamer and add the chicken breast. Peel the carrots and cut into 10 cm (3″) sticks. Wash and string the snow peas. Put the carrots on the other side of the steamer. Don't add the snow peas yet.

When the water comes to a boil, place the steamer in the pot, cover and cook for about 8 minutes. Then add snow peas and cook for another 2 or 3 minutes. Remove from heat. Don't overcook or you will dry out the chicken.

While the chicken and bulghur are cooking, prepare some Light Sauce (p. 56) and mince 6 or 7 sprigs of parsley. Pour the puréed pears into 2 dessert bowls; peel and cut fresh pears into quarters and place on top of the purée. Set aside.

When the chicken is cooked, slice thinly and serve with bulghur sprinkled with parsley. Surround with the cooked vegetables and pour on the sauce.

4

Eating Out

Women are eating out more than ever before: teenagers are addicted to fast food, women executives are invited to power breakfasts or obliged to host business lunches, housewives are looking for a break from the kitchen, older women are seeking a change of scenery. Nearly all women eat away from home at least a few times a week. Some even eat out twice a day! Forty per cent of breakfast eaters in restaurants are women and one out of seven business travelers is a woman.

This trend toward eating fewer meals at home is not necessarily what women want. The pleasure of being served is somewhat spoiled by the challenge of finding health-conscious restaurants that serve adequate portions of nutritious food. The more often women eat out, the more they tend to complain about the meals, because they rarely find daily specials that suit their particular needs.

The problem is not the occasional fancy dinner party, but rather the day-to-day accumulation of unbalanced lunches and dinners. People tend to eat differently in restaurants than they do at home. According to a recent U.S. study, three out of five consumers are concerned about the nutritive value of their diet when they're at home, but only two out of five care about it in restaurants! Data shows a tendency toward eating less healthy foods in restaurants: more french fries and soft drinks; fewer vegetables and fruits.

The popularity of certain restaurant foods indicates that while health concerns have made a lot of headway, they don't always top consumers' lists of priorities. Restaurants have never offered so many low-sodium dishes, smaller portions, decaffeinated coffee, fruit, salads, and juice, yet orders for french fries, "diet" soft drinks, desserts, and all-you-can-eat buffets have also reached record highs.

EATING OUT: THE PITFALLS

Although nutritional analyses do not exist for every type of meal served in restaurants, there is enough information available for women to be able to correct certain shortcomings. We do know that meals eaten in restaurants contain fewer nutrients than meals eaten at home, but we still don't know the reason for this discrepancy. Do consumers make poor choices or is it that many restaurants lack a wide enough selection?

Fast-food restaurant meals are generally low in calcium, vitamin C, vitamin A, magnesium, thiamin, and fiber, but high in protein, fat, and calories. A teenage girl who eats a lot of fast food can compensate for shortcomings by choosing the right snacks: milk, yogurt, fruit, or a bran muffin.

The trendy new "croissant restaurants" springing up everywhere are really no cause for celebration. A croissant with ham, for instance, has twice as many calories and double the fat of a fried chicken breast! Women would be far better off with a conventional sandwich, especially if made with whole-grain bread.

Salad bars, which attract many "thin-conscious" patrons, can also be deceptive. An analysis of twelve salad meals chosen by students on a U.S. campus revealed that half of the salads contained up to 1,000 calories and more fat than six of the hot meals served at the same cafeteria! The ingredients responsible for this dietary disaster were not the greens or raw vegetables, but rather all the extras such as bacon bits, strips of cheese, cold cuts, olives, and salad dressing! Women who are looking for a light meal at a salad bar must be selective (see page 64).

Many restaurants offer special business lunches every day. An analysis of the nutrient content of these meals at twenty-five Montreal restaurants showed that the portions served were too high in calories, containing a particularly unhealthy amount of fat and low nutrient value for women.

The classic "steak, potatoes, bread, and salad" choice is just not the best bet for women. A study showed that this type of meal, whether served in a fancy restaurant or a snack bar, provides an average of 1,400 calories, a large amount of fat, and not enough iron or calcium to meet even a third of a woman's daily requirements. How many women can allow themselves to eat 1,400 calories in a single meal? Fat and calories could be cut by reducing the serving of meat to 100 g (3 1/2 oz) but iron and calcium requirements would have to be made up at some other meal or snack.

It seems that the more men and women eat out, the more likely they are to affect negatively the nutritive value of their diet. The more a *woman* eats out, the greater the nutrition challenge she faces. Women not only have to demand smaller portions but must also compensate for the lack of calcium, iron, and vitamin B$_6$ in most restaurant menus.

Best Choices

Some restaurants do offer health-conscious menus. However, even if nutritious foods make up most of the menu (salads, fish, fruit), whole grains (whole-wheat bread, brown rice, whole-wheat pasta) may be absent.

If you eat out often, improve your choices to feel as good after the meal as before and to fulfill nutritional needs. The best strategy is to reduce portions of high-fat foods (meat, cheese, dishes with a lot of sauce) to leave more room for vitamin and mineral-rich foods (vegetables, fruit, whole grains). Be particularly careful at lunchtime and try not to fall into the most common traps: a heavy and hard-to-digest business lunch, or a meal so light that you will lack the energy to finish your day.

If you eat out regularly and would like to increase the amount of vitamins, minerals, and fiber in your diet, while reducing your fat intake:

1. Order spring water with a twist of lemon or vegetable juice instead of an aperitif; splurge occasionally with a spritzer (half soda, half white wine). Avoid wine at lunch.

2. Order an appetizer made with vegetables, unless your main course is vegetable soup or a salad.

Order:

Green salad
Vegetable juice
Vegetable terrine
Raw vegetable plate
Vegetable soup
Carrot salad
Celery remoulade
Tomato slices with tarragon or basil
Leeks vinaigrette
Ask for vinaigrette on the side, so you can add as much—or as little—as you like.

3. Don't skip bread, especially if it's whole-wheat or dark rye. Eat it without butter as often as possible. You can choose melba toast instead of bread, but it contains fewer nutrients. Croissants contain as much fat as two and a half pats of butter. Save them for a special occasion!

4. Avoid high-fat or high-protein appetizers unless your main course is a vegetable salad.

Avoid:

Meat pâté
Meat terrine
Pâté de foie gras
Shrimp cocktail
Fish entrées
Coquilles Saint-Jacques
Spring rolls

5. Whenever possible, especially at lunchtime, ask for a half portion of your main course. Portion size is usually designed for men, not women! Don't be shy about asking for a half portion, if that is all you can or want to eat. Alternately, order two nutritious and complementary appetizers.

Give top priority to broiled or poached fish, seafood bro-

chettes, boiled lobster, shellfish served plain, or "marinara"—
in a vegetable or wine-based sauce instead of cream sauce.

Order broiled or poached chicken.

At least once a week, eat broiled liver or braised kidney
for a meal that is super-rich in iron.

Ask that sauce be served on the side.

For Lunches on the Run:

Eat a sandwich on whole-wheat bread or pita, filled with chicken,
salmon, tuna, egg, humus, or lentils. If you like, you can specify
no butter or mayonnaise.

Order just the salad bar. Concentrate on greens and add
hard-boiled eggs or cottage cheese, chickpeas and kidney beans
for protein.

Eat a small vegetable, cheese, or seafood pizza.

Avoid pizza with pepperoni, anchovies, smoked meat, or
bacon.

Order an appetizer rather than a main-course serving of
fresh pasta with a vegetable or seafood sauce.

Order a poached egg Florentine served on a bed of spinach
with a couple of slices of whole-wheat toast.

6. Choose your side dishes carefully.

Order:	**Instead of:**
Boiled or baked potato	French fries
Plain vegetables	Vegetables in sauce or fried
Steamed rice	Fried rice
Salad	Pickles

7. End your meal with a light dessert, if you really must have
dessert.

Order:

A fresh apple or pear
A dish of fresh ripe strawberries in season
A slice of fresh pineapple
A bunch of grapes

A kiwi cut in half; eat with a spoon
A slice of watermelon
A quarter cantaloupe
Fresh fruit salad—or, if not available:
A mixture of fresh and canned fruit
Fruit sherbet or fruit ice
Applesauce

If your meal is just soup, a cooked vegetable plate, or a vegetable salad, order a dessert that provides some protein:

Yogurt
Cheese
Crème caramel
Ice cream

8. End your meal with coffee (regular or decaffeinated) or herbal tea, but avoid black or green tea which inhibits the absorption of iron, one of the most vulnerable nutrients in a woman's diet.

PACKING YOUR OWN LUNCH

Many women prefer to bring their own lunch to work. Home-made lunches have a number of advantages: they're half the price of restaurant meals and there's no waiting to be served. Brown-bag lunches are infinitely adaptable . . . from the meeting room to a park bench or even a lunchtime concert! There's no limit to what you can pack for lunch. You can eat healthy foods to your heart's content. Let your imagination run wild! But if you want your lunch to pay dividends, you must treat it like a proper meal:

- Never eat while you work. A meal that is gulped down un-noticed will not meet your physical or spiritual needs.
- Don't eat at your desk or work station. A change of scenery will do you good.
- Lay out your lunch on a place mat or a linen napkin that you can keep in your drawer or cupboard.
- Use real plates and cutlery instead of cardboard, paper, or plastic.

- Experiment! Add new flavors to your lunch to turn a routine meal into a surprise.
- Plan a collective meal once a week. Share the work and expense with your co-workers. One can bring the vegetables, another the bread, a third the fruit or dessert. Make mealtime a social event again!
- For a healthy last-minute lunch, take a trip to a supermarket that has a salad counter: design yourself a salad, add a yogurt, a bran muffin, and a tin of vegetable juice.
- A 15-minute walk before going back to work will help you digest your lunch.

It's not hard to make a last-minute lunch at home if you have good food on hand. All you have to do is fill the fridge and pantry once a week with easy-to-prepare or even ready-to-eat foods:

- Dairy products: individual servings of yogurt and cheese, small milk cartons.
- Grains: stock the freezer with whole-grain bread. Choose whole-wheat rolls, oatmeal or dark rye bread, whole-wheat pita, bran muffins.
- Meat and alternates (why limit yourself to ham and processed meats?): cooked chicken, canned salmon or tuna, cooked fish fillets, frozen or canned crab, fresh, frozen or canned shrimp, canned chickpeas and kidney beans, eggs, nuts, or nut butter.
- Fruit: apples, pears, peaches, grapes, oranges, mandarin oranges, and clementines travel best.
- Vegetables: fresh spinach is a good substitute for tired iceberg lettuce. Or use romaine. Try alfalfa sprouts, watercress, or endive; buy some tomato juice or vegetable juice in small cans or drinking boxes, eat more raw vegetables than usual; buy some shiny green or red peppers for crunchy snacking, some regular or cherry tomatoes.
- Treats for dessert or before lunch, to quell any hunger pangs: dried dates, figs, apricots, almonds, hazelnuts, sunflower seeds.

Give leftovers a new lease on life! Cook once and serve twice. Why not cook one or two extra servings for supper so you'll have enough left over for lunches?

- Leftover cooked meat or chicken can make a tasty salad or sandwich or go into the soup pot.
- Cooked fish can be mixed with light mayonnaise, minced green onion, pepper strips, and tomato quarters for a delicious salad.
- Leftover cooked vegetables (broccoli, cauliflower, green beans, carrots, zucchini, snow peas) can be mixed with raw vegetables like peppers, celery, and green onions. Voilà! A supersalad with panache!
- That extra ratatouille can be eaten cold or added to fresh or leftover cooked pasta to make a salad that's a meal in itself.
- Make up a batch of homemade vinaigrette; it travels very well in small spice bottles.
- Leftover cooked pasta makes an excellent salad with the addition of some vinaigrette, cooked and/or raw vegetables, chunks of chicken, seafood, or half a cup of chickpeas.
- Yesterday's brown rice or cooked barley, sprinkled with vinaigrette, a liberal amount of chopped parsley and green onion, thyme and pepper chunks is great with a slice or two of cooked meat or a piece of cheese.
- Any washed salad greens left over from supper can be placed in a small plastic bag for the next day's lunch; add a little vinaigrette just before eating.
- Leftover fruit jellies travel well.
- Dress up a serving of last evening's fruit salad with an apple, cut into chunks, and a few walnuts.
- Applesauce keeps well. Mix it with equal parts of plain yogurt and some raisins for a delicious dessert.

A packed lunch is a balanced meal if it contains foods that provide different nutrients. A lunch consisting of vegetable soup, raw vegetable sticks, green salad, and fruit is not balanced. Although there are four different dishes, all four contain the same nutrients. A balanced meal contains:

- At least one serving of vegetable and one of fruit.
- At least one whole-grain product: whole-wheat bread, brown rice, barley, and the like.
- A small portion of meat, poultry, fish, tofu, or cooked legumes.
- A dairy product: carton of milk, yogurt, or cheese which can be dessert or a snack.

WOMEN ON THE MOVE

More and more women are traveling on business these days—as noted previously, the ratio is one woman to six men. These women cannot afford to neglect their diet if they want to keep up their energy level.

Traveling today is challenging enough without having a series of strict dietary rules to follow. The point is to adopt eating habits that will make the difference between coming home feeling good—even ready for another trip—or arriving home ready to collapse!

I travel extensively in Canada, the United States, and Europe, sometimes giving two lectures and three interviews in two days. Here are some golden rules that keep me at my best:

1. Never skip a meal. Get up earlier if you must, or cut short a meeting, but never miss a chance to eat. Meals are an opportunity to relax, regain your strength, and refuel!
2. Turn down a glass of wine or a drink because nothing is as tiring as alcohol. Many women have trouble tolerating alcohol even under normal circumstances. If you want to handle the stress of traveling, you can't add another source of fatigue. My advice is not to drink at all—not even moderately.
3. Give priority to the very best foods, no matter where you are eating. Each day, try to eat:
   • At least 175 g (6 oz) yogurt and 45 g (1 1/2 oz) cheese *or* drink an 8-oz carton of milk.
   • At least one bowl of bran cereal or a bran muffin and a few slices of whole-wheat bread.
   • Two small servings (90 g or 3 oz) broiled meat, fish, or chicken.
   • At least half a grapefruit, an orange, a green salad, and a serving of broccoli or cauliflower.

If you are traveling in a country where only white bread is served, pack some fiber biscuits in your suitcase and eat at least two a day (you can buy these biscuits at the drugstore).

The foods suggested above are easy to find and full of the best nutrients. Your menu could look like this:

• Breakfast: half a grapefruit, bran muffin, and yogurt or a glass of milk.

- Lunch: green salad, chicken sandwich on whole-wheat bread, an orange.
- Supper: glass of tomato juice, small fillet of broiled fish, boiled potato, broccoli, whole-wheat bread.
- Bedtime or snack: cheese or a glass of milk.

Productive Snacks

When hunger strikes, when meetings drag on, and when meals have to wait . . . don't hesitate to snack on something healthy. Contrary to popular belief, your body works much better if you snack than if you fast.

- Your body uses calories better when you eat a number of small meals. Experiments with people wanting to lose weight have shown that the metabolism burns calories more efficiently when they are ingested evenly over the day than when they are consumed in one or two large meals.
- The calcium in food is absorbed better when taken in small amounts.

Good snacks pay dividends when they supply vitamins and minerals with every bite! They are not hard to find. Many vending machines sell:

- Sunflower seeds
- Mixed nuts
- Plain or fruit yogurt
- Small cartons of milk
- Cheese and crackers
- Fresh fruit
- Vegetable juice

Home-made snacks are great too:

- Plain almonds
- Mixed dried fruit and nuts
- Engevita or torula yeast. Add 15 to 30 mL (1 or 2 tbsp) to a small glass of water or milk.

For each bite to count, make the most of every eating opportunity, including snacks.

Anti-Jet-Lag Formula

Have you ever felt completely drained after a very long continental or overseas flight? Have you ever been in Paris or Hawaii and been starving three hours before or after meals but not at mealtimes? Have you ever dreamed of arriving at your destination feeling synchronized with local time?

This is what Dr. Charles Ehret of Illinois had in mind when he came up with his anti-jet-lag formula. I've used this schedule and highly recommend it to all women who travel on business or for pleasure and who hate to waste time feeling out-of-sorts. It's really very simple.

1. Find out the day and time of breakfast at your destination and start to follow the schedule four days before. (If you are leaving for Europe on Saturday night, start the schedule on Wednesday morning, or four days before your first overseas breakfast, Sunday morning at 8 a.m.).
2. Call your travel agent and order lacto-vegetarian meals for the flight. Before leaving, confirm the order at the ticket counter.
3. In the four days prior to the flight, alternate between a "feast" day and a "fast" day; the day you leave must always be a fast day (see menus, below).
4. On "feast" days, eat a high-protein breakfast and lunch; in the evening, eat a high-starch meal.
5. On "fast" days, eat fruits and vegetables, a small amount of grain products at every meal, and as little fat as possible (no butter on your bread, hardly any vinaigrette on your salad).
6. During the flight, drink a lot of water, fruit or vegetable juice; avoid regular coffee after the evening meal; avoid all alcohol. Drinking wine or other alcohol at an altitude of 8,000 meters is very dehydrating and will be three times more tiring than on the ground.
7. Try to sleep until breakfasttime at your destination, then eat a high-protein meal. Ask for one or two yogurts or cheese if only rolls and jam are served. Don't sleep after breakfast. Stay awake until you arrive at your destination. Once you get there, eat at local meal times and avoid snoozing until after dinner. (A nap before dinner could ruin the whole plan!)

SUGGESTED MENU FOR "FEAST" DAYS (DAYS 1 AND 3)

Breakfast:
Fruit, poached egg or cheese, bread *or* fruit, cereal with chopped nuts and milk
Lunch:
Green salad, broiled chicken, bread, fruit *or* vegetable juice, poached fish and rice, fruit
Dinner:
Green salad, pasta with tomato sauce, dessert (fruit) *or* raw vegetable sticks, rice pilaf with vegetables, bread, dessert (fruit)

SUGGESTED MENU FOR "FAST" DAYS (DAYS 2 AND 4)

Breakfast:
As much fruit as you like, bran muffin or toast *or* cereal, milk, fruit
Lunch and Dinner:
Green salad, cooked vegetable plate, bread, fruit *or* raw vegetable sticks, vegetable soup, bread and fruit

If the four-day schedule seems too complicated, at least try to follow the instructions for the flight: lacto-vegetarian meals, lots of water or juice, and *no alcohol.*

5

Living Alone

More people live alone today than ever before. The majority are women; many are young, many more are elderly. Studies reveal that the proportion of women 65 and over living alone has doubled in the last quarter century.

Women who live alone may have chosen to do so or may have been forced into the situation as a result of separation, divorce, or widowhood. *The less agreeable this solitude to an individual, the greater its negative effects.* One of the worst negative effects is a deterioration in eating habits. It seems that eating alone can be even more of a problem than living alone!

Many women living alone forget to do the grocery shopping, don't feel like cooking, or waste good food bought on impulse. It's not surprising, then, that they are often lacking important nutrients. Other women fill the void by eating . . . and eating . . . and eating. Still others lose their appetite or even their desire to go on living. They see meals as social events and without someone to share with, eating loses all of its appeal.

A young woman used to eating with the family may not feel like eating when she moves out and finds herself alone at the table all the time.

An older woman who has spent her whole life looking after others, keeping an eye on their health and diet, may not feel like eating when she no longer has children or a husband to feed.

A grandmother who lives alone in a small apartment may not have enough space to invite her children and grandchildren over for meals.

Some women who have learned to live alone without losing their interest in food have helped me develop eating strategies that have as much to do with the atmosphere in which the meal is served as its content. These women have developed a good relationship with food in their own way.

ENVIABLE FREEDOM

Women who live alone often forget the benefits they enjoy.

They are free of the responsibility of feeding a hungry family as soon as they set foot in the door—a freedom many working mothers would envy.

They can go anywhere they wish at mealtime without calling a summit meeting. They can replace a meal with a nutritious snack without having to listen to snide comments. They can even forget to come home without being interrogated!

Women who live alone are free to participate in sports or take fitness classes whenever it suits them. They can take their own time to eat whatever they like, whenever they like, and however they like!

A Comfortable Place to Eat

Some women who live alone like to sit down quietly at the table, and eat with no distractions. Others opt for a comfortable corner of the living room or for a small folding table or a tray in the bedroom rather than looking at an empty table and chairs. Others time their meals to coincide with a favorite radio or television program; they prefer this to silence.

Rules for family dinners no longer apply to women living on their own. Finding a daily routine that pleases you is very important. It will stimulate your appetite and add to your eating pleasure.

Treat Yourself Right

Women programmed to please others often forget to please themselves! After devoting all their attention to family and friends, they tend to neglect themselves, meal after meal.

- Why not serve yourself as good a meal as you would serve your friends?
- Why not take the time to sit down and eat and enjoy your meal, even if it's only cheese, a few slices of bread, and some vegetable sticks?
- Why not eat with a beautiful plant, some flowers, or a favorite piece of music as company? Why not light a candle or two to give your dinner a festive air?
- Why not buy something special that you like: fresh lobster, smoked salmon, fillet of trout, filet mignon, an artichoke, an endive, or a special sherbet or ice cream?
- Why not open a half bottle of wine occasionally if that adds to your eating pleasure?
- Why wait for company to eat at a beautifully set and decorated table?

NO-FRILLS ENTERTAINING

The more you invite people over for dinner, the more invitations you'll receive, but this can be a double-edged sword. To benefit from this exchange you must learn to entertain without frills! This applies to all women, but particularly to those who live alone and are lonely, but hesitate to make a fuss about entertaining.

To simplify your entertaining, forget all about complicated recipes, lavishly decorated tables, impeccable housekeeping and concentrate on the social aspect. Invite people over at the last minute because you feel like eating with someone, not because you feel like cooking! The menus below illustrate what I mean.

FOUR SEASONS MENU

Rôtisserie chicken
Green salad
Hot rolls
Fresh fruit in season

WINTER MENU

Macaroni and cheese
Pepper rings vinaigrette

Melba toast or toast
Applesauce and cinnamon

FOUR SEASONS MENU

Soup
Cheese
Whole-grain bread
Fresh grapes

SUMMER MENU

Quiche
Ripe tomato slices sprinkled with chopped fresh herbs: chives,
parsley, basil, or tarragon
Whole-wheat pita
Quarter cantaloupe and strawberry sherbet

Entertaining can be fun even if you aren't a great cook! A little
initiative is all it takes. Invite a neighbor or co-worker, or anyone
else whose company you enjoy. The less complicated it is, the
less you'll hesitate about entertaining, and the less often you'll
be alone! When you really feel like cooking, go for it! Prepare
an extra-large quantity of macaroni, meat loaf, spaghetti sauce,
or lasagna and freeze the surplus in individual servings. Roast
a chicken for tasty leftovers. Or prepare a small roast of beef.

SHOPPING FOR ONE

Shopping before mealtime whets the appetite and will help you
fill your shopping cart. There's no magic formula for all women,
but the following tips should be helpful:

1. Buy small packages to prevent leftovers and waste.

• Vegetable juice in 200-mL (6-oz) containers.
• Salmon and tuna in 100- or 200-g (3-1/2 or 6-2/3 oz) tins.
• Fresh boneless skinless chicken breast.
• Yogurt in 125- or 175-g (4- or 6-oz) containers.

- Individually wrapped servings of cheese.
- Single muffins, cakes, or cookies.
- Small boxes of cereal.
- Applesauce in single-serving cans.
- Unsweetened puréed fruit in 128-mL jars (tasty over plain yogurt or on toast).
- Ask the clerk at the meat or fish counter for small portions (90 to 100 g (3 or 4 oz)) of liver, fish, or seafood.

2. Buying some frozen foods also helps prevent waste:

- Frozen vegetables such as broccoli, cauliflower, spinach, corn in 250- or 300-g (8- or 10-oz) packages.
- Frozen dinners (see pages 39 and 47).
- Frozen unsweetened strawberries and raspberries in 300-g (10-oz) packages.
- Frozen bran waffles for a special breakfast.
- Individually wrapped frozen fish fillets.
- Frozen shrimp or scallops in small bags (use only what you need and put the rest in the freezer).

If you live alone, you have the same nutritional requirements as any other woman your age. To meet all your protein, vitamin, and mineral requirements, you should eat the following every day:

- At least three servings of fruit
- At least three servings of vegetables
- At least four servings of grain products
- At least three servings of dairy products
- A good source of protein at each meal, including meat or a good alternate at lunch and supper

Here's a shopping list which meets all the nutritional requirements of an adult woman who eats all her meals at home. Teenagers, pregnant women, or nursing mothers should add one serving of dairy products and one serving of grain products each day and increase all the other servings as desired.

Weekly Shopping List

For three servings of fruit per day:

- six oranges (6 servings)
- one grapefruit (2 servings)
- one small cantaloupe or honeydew melon
- three bananas (3 servings)
- frozen strawberries, 300-g/10-oz package (3 servings)

For three servings of vegetables per day:

- frozen broccoli, 250-g/8-oz package (3 servings)
- frozen spinach, 250-g/8-oz package (3 servings)
- one bunch of fresh carrots (4 servings)
- one Boston or romaine lettuce (3 to 4 servings)
- two cans or bottles of vegetable juice, 200-mL/6-oz (2 servings)
- one large can of tomatoes (4 servings)

During the summer, be sure to buy your vegetables fresh at your local farmers' market!

For four servings of grain products per day plus some left over:

- one whole-wheat loaf/(450 g/15 oz) (14 slices)
- 250 g (1/2 lb) brown rice (8 servings)
- 450 g (1 lb) whole-wheat pasta (about 10 servings)
- one box of shredded wheat cereal (6 servings)

For three servings of dairy products per day:

- two liters of milk (8 servings)
- seven individual yogurts (7 servings)
- 250 g (1/2 lb) cheese (8 servings)

For two meat or meat substitute meals per day:

- 100-g (3-1/2 oz) can salmon (1 serving)
- six eggs (4 or 5 per week)
- 1 can of kidney beans, 450-mL can (3 or 4 servings)
- 100 g (3 1/2 oz) calves' liver (1 serving)

- two frozen fish or chicken dinners (see suggestions on p. 39) (2 servings)
- 1 skinless boneless chicken breast (2 servings)

Women who eat one whole meal per day at a restaurant should subtract the equivalent of seven servings of each food group from the list.

Pantry for All Seasons

Well-stocked cupboards are the perfect solution for unexpected visitors and balanced meals.

1. Keep basic seasonings for salad dressings, sauces, soups, and desserts on hand:

- Virgin olive oil for salads
- Sunflower or corn oil for cooking and baking
- Cider or wine vinegar for salads
- Vegetable bouillon cubes
- Canned chicken broth and consommé
- Salt and pepper
- Thyme, oregano, basil, and any other dried herbs you choose
- Tamari sauce (natural soya sauce)
- Mixed dried herbs
- Dijon mustard
- Honey, white or brown sugar
- Cinnamon, nutmeg, ginger, and other spices of choice
- *Pure* vanilla extract, if possible.

2. Basic ingredients for everyday meals:

- All-purpose whole-wheat flour
- Baking powder
- Baking soda
- Wheat germ (keep it in the fridge)
- Natural bran to add fiber to your meals (use instead of bread crumbs)
- Brown rice
- Whole-wheat pasta
- Rolled oats (not instant)

- Unflavored gelatin (packets or sheets)
- Peanut butter or other nut butter
- Herbal teas
- Coffee and tea

3. Ingredients to have on hand for special-occasion meals, or drop-in visitors, or for emergency situations:

- Canned salmon or tuna
- Canned sardines
- Canned beans (chickpeas, kidney beans)
- Dried lentils (for a good soup)
- Skim milk powder
- Evaporated milk
- Canned tomatoes
- Canned cream of vegetable soups or packaged soup mixes
- Small containers of vegetable juice
- Small containers of fruit juice
- Dried fruit
- Nuts in the shell or sunflower seeds
- Unsweetened applesauce in small containers

4. Keep on hand in the freezer for holidays or impromptu meals:

- A few frozen dinners (see p. 47)
- Frozen vegetables of your choice
- Frozen unsweetened orange juice
- Frozen individually wrapped fish fillets
- Unsweetened frozen fruit
- Whole-wheat bread or rolls
- Bran muffins or biscuits

Useful Appliances

Nothing beats good tools and good organization, whether you live alone or not! Some appliances, like a food processor and a microwave oven, can reduce preparation and cooking time.

Food processors make it easy to prepare soups, sauces, milkshakes, purées, and coulises (fruit sauces). A microwave[1]

---

(1) Microwave ovens are not dangerous; cooking food in the microwave has nothing to do with food irradiation. Microwaves penetrate the food and cause

is a boon for fast last-minute meals, defrosting and heating left-overs, and warming frozen dinners. It keeps dirty dishes to a minimum and works fastest with small quantities. Foods cooked or reheated in the microwave retain their vitamins and minerals as well or better than traditionally cooked foods. Vegetables cooked in the microwave require a minimum of water and retain more vitamin C than when steamed.

LETTING OTHERS DO THE COOKING

There may be some dishes that you like to eat, but don't feel like cooking when you live alone: coquilles Saint-Jacques, lamb or liver shish kebab, pasta with a complex sauce, lasagna, a delicious but complicated vegetarian dish, salad with unusual greens, crêpes, even a bran muffin. . . . If you want to treat yourself to the special dish you crave:

- Choose a restaurant that specializes in the dish you are dying to eat and that will provide a table for one. Bring along a newspaper or a book to enjoy once you've finished reading the menu.
- Invite a friend to share a meal at a restaurant. A main-course dish is often enough for two women! Order a soup or salad each. For a limited investment, you can both have a good meal.
- Try out the prepared food counter at the supermarket or your neighborhood caterer. Watch for vacuum-packed meals which will soon be revolutionizing the ready-to-eat market.
- Ask a friend or relative who also likes that special dish to prepare an extra-large quantity and freeze some for you. Have a good visit when you go to pick it up!

---

the molecules to move faster. That's what heats the food. Irradiation, on the other hand, is a process that uses cobalt 60 gamma rays to sterilize food before it is sold. It can result in the loss of certain nutrients and the appearance of radiolytic components. The long-term effect of food irradiation on human health is not yet known. For irradiated foods to be sold in Canada, a special label is required. Health and Welfare Canada are unaware of any being available to the public at this time.

THE DESCHENE SOLUTION

A grandmother I know explained how she entertains her grand-children despite her small apartment. I was so impressed by her idea that I named it after her.

Grandma Deschêne organizes parties from time to time at her grown children's homes, usually from 5 to 8 p.m. Mme Deschêne chooses the date, does the shopping, cooks some of the food at her house, buys some good wine, and brings it all with her. She arrives at about five o'clock, finishes the last-minute preparations, and enjoys her grandchildren. As a bonus they tend to eat better and behave better when they're in their own surroundings! When bath and bedtime rolls around, Grandma Deschêne collects her belongings and returns home to the peace and quiet of her own apartment!

MORE TIPS

Check the list of good last-minute foods and meals (page 47) and tips on eating out (page 62), which are also useful for women who live alone.

Small Appetites, Small Meals

When you're not very hungry and don't have much energy, it's far better to eat something small than nothing at all. The following dishes take next to no time to make and are very good for you!

MUFFIN À LA MODE

Makes 1 serving

1 bran muffin
125 g (1/2 cup) plain yogurt
125 g (1/2 cup) unsweetened pear purée

1 tbsp wheat germ
2 tbsp ground almonds

Cut the muffin in half and place in a bowl or on a plate. Combine the other ingredients and pour over it.

Variations

To increase the calcium content, replace the almonds with freshly ground sesame seeds.
    Instead of pear purée, try applesauce.
    For 3 more grams of protein, add 1 tbsp engevita yeast.

MAGIC SOUFFLÉ

Makes 1 or 2 servings

2 slices whole-wheat bread
Butter
60 g (2 oz) mild cheese, grated
1 egg
200 mL (6 oz) milk
Salt and pepper to taste

Butter the slices of bread. Place one slice in a small ovenproof dish and sprinkle with half the grated cheese. Top with the other slice of bread and remaining cheese.
    Beat egg with milk; add salt and pepper to taste. Pour over bread. Bake at 350°F for about 25 minutes.
    Serve with a few slices of tomato or other raw vegetables.

MINUTE MINESTRONE

Makes 3 or 4 small meals
(This recipe is easy to make and leftovers can be frozen. Add the cheese just before serving.)

1 28-oz can tomatoes (about 800 mL)
1 400-g or 540-mL can kidney beans, well drained

1 finely chopped green onion or chopped chives
Pinch of dried thyme
Salt and pepper to taste
Grated cheese, about 30 g (1 oz) per serving

Pour tomatoes into a pot, crush with a fork, or cut with two knives. Add green onion or chives and thyme. Simmer for a few minutes. Add kidney beans and heat. Pour into a soup bowl and sprinkle generously with grated cheese.

Serve with a slice of toast or a whole-wheat roll.

HOT CEREAL SUPREME

Makes 1 serving

90 g (3/4 cup) rolled oats (regular)
2 tbsp bran
1 tbsp wheat germ
250 mL (1 cup) apple juice
125 g (1/2 cup) vanilla yogurt
A few toasted chopped almonds, optional

Heat the apple juice in a small pot. Combine rolled oats, bran, and wheat germ. Add to the hot apple juice and cook as directed. Serve in a bowl with a generous dollop of vanilla yogurt. Sprinkle with toasted almonds if desired.

Accompany with fresh fruit.

MEAL IN A GLASS

Makes 1 large serving

200 mL (6 oz) part-skim milk
1 small banana
1 egg
30 mL (2 tbsp) frozen orange juice concentrate
1 tbsp wheat germ

Combine all ingredients in blender or food processor. Pour into a large glass. Drink slowly!

6

Unconventional Diets

I have seen many women become tired and depressed after opting for a meatless menu or an unconventional diet. Many have become interested in macrobiotics or "food combination" approaches. Others have lost confidence in the traditional "food guide" and feel their health is at stake.

The more anxious people become about their health, the more fad diets appear on the market, and the greater the margin for error—all in the name of "healthier eating". Women are more vulnerable than ever when it comes to nutrition and they already have enough trouble meeting their dietary needs, without imposing new restrictions on their food choices. They simply don't have the luxury of trying out dead-end solutions.

Let's take a brief look at how nutrition consciousness has evolved in North America over the past forty years so as to gain some insight into the current situation.

After the food shortages of the Second World War, the 1950s glorified the new abundance, adopted a carefree attitude about food, and promoted calorie-laden recipes. North Americans happily downed fried eggs, bacon, buttered white bread spread thickly with jam, coffee with cream, and lots of sugar. Although books by the well-known American nutritionist Adele Davis were widely read, nutrition itself was not a hot topic in those days. It was a growing science, but it still interested few people outside the lab.

In the 1960s, large steaks (6 oz or more), fried foods, soft drinks, and sweet desserts were very popular. Modern health problems reached their peak at about the same time. Unhealthy eating habits still had not been targeted as a cause; nutritionists had not yet established the link between diet and the incidence of certain diseases. In those days, natural food "freaks" were among the very few who advocated eating unprocessed, unrefined foods for a healthier diet and lifestyle.

A few studies published in the early 1970s established a relationship between diet and disease. These studies immediately led to an information revolution. Organizations began spreading the word about preventing heart attacks, cancer, and high blood pressure through improved nutrition. Although all this advice was aimed at better health, the messages differed. One organization stressed reducing salt intake, while another focused only on fiber. Some groups battled animal fat. Others attacked all fats. Then the war broke out between butter and margarine. Foods were divided into two camps: foods that caused disease—and all the others; foods that could be eaten without guilt—and the rest. The number of natural food fans and vegetarians multiplied by millions.

The 1980s became the decade of confusion. Studies continued to arouse a great deal of interest. Nutrition information campaigns, some conducted by health agencies and others by different food industries, attracted attention but trumpeted conflicting messages. Consumers have never worked harder to improve their food habits, but they have also lost confidence in their food. They have become confused. Women still worry more than men because they feel responsible for the health of their loved ones. Food is undeniably one of the keys to good health, but it no longer offers the security it used to. Ensuring good nutrition seems to have become more complex than ever.

There has never been a better time to propose a diet that can guarantee wellness. But some diets are so strict that they increase anxiety or even cause new dietary imbalances. Some people have become "nutritionists" on the strength of a "cure" and promote their new way of eating at every opportunity. Here's a look at some of the diets that have become popular in recent years.

FOOD COMBINATIONS

The food combination theory was developed by Herbert Shelton about thirty years ago and has been taken up again recently by the authors of *Fit for Life*. This diet calls for eating designated groups of foods in specific combinations.

The daily menu plan calls for eating fruit in the morning, protein and vegetables for lunch, grains and vegetables for dinner. According to this diet, you must avoid eating starch with meat, green vegetables with fruit, milk with grains, an orange with a banana, or an apple and yogurt at the same meal. Fruit can be eaten only at the beginning of a meal; melon must be eaten on its own.

Shelton, who directed a health school in Texas in the 1950s, had hoped that his diet would cure digestive problems, but he did not foresee the side effects it would have. His food combination menus have become synonymous with complicated, poorly adapted, and unbalanced meals: an analysis of fifteen of these daily menus reveals a serious shortage of calories, protein, zinc, vitamin B_{12}, calcium, and vitamin D. And any advantages there may be in digesting one type of food at a time are soon annulled by loss of energy, muscle tone, and even hair.

Shelton based his theory on only one digestive enzyme: ptyalin, a salivary enzyme that starts the digestive process of cooked low-fiber starches but which cannot even act on whole grains. He developed his whole eating strategy on the premise that it was possible to slow down the normal digestive process of at least ten other enzymes that work in sequence, regardless of the menu. But he forgot that the whole set of enzymes, whether they be acid or alkaline, are stimulated by the introduction of food to the mouth—regardless of whether it is a piece of meat or fruit. Although Shelton did recommend eating nutritious foods, he forgot that if certain foods are eaten separately, it is more difficult for the body to retain their best properties. For example, protein is best absorbed when eaten with starch. Iron is best absorbed with vitamin C.

A woman who adopts this eating strategy will no longer be meeting her nutritional requirements. She will lose weight because she is not fully absorbing the food she is eating separately. She may become exhausted after a few months because the suggested menus do not provide enough protein.

After meeting many women who had become weakened and even ill because of this diet, I realized that I could not remain silent. Food combinations seriously restrict the number of foods that can be eaten and inhibit the absorption of important nutrients. People who choose to eat fruit before their meals on the basis of this diet have nothing to worry about, but those who follow Shelton's theories to the letter for a long period of time may do themselves serious harm.

VEGETARIANISM

There is nothing new about vegetarianism. The only novelty is when we see former meat-eaters becoming passionate about grains and greens!

In industrialized countries, many meat-eaters convert to vegetarianism because of its respect for ecological balance and for health reasons. Thriftiness, the love of animals, and a spiritual dimension are other motivating factors. First there are the *strict vegetarians* or *vegans*, who refuse to eat any foods of animal origin: dairy products, eggs, gelatin, chicken broth, and the like.

Lacto-ovo-vegetarians eat no meat, chicken, or fish, but they do drink milk and eat cheese, yogurt, and eggs.

Then there are those who avoid red meat but who will occasionally eat fish or chicken. They are called *semi-vegetarians*.

The challenge for all vegetarians is to eat enough good-quality protein to build, maintain, and repair the body's tissues, muscles, bones, skin, hair, and so on. The advantages of a balanced vegetarian diet are, however, scientifically proven:

• A vegetarian diet is generally lower in saturated fats and higher in dietary fiber. As a result, vegetarians usually have lower cholesterol levels, fewer cardiovascular problems, and are less likely to suffer from constipation.
• This type of diet often provides more potassium and magnesium. Vegetarians often have much lower blood pressure than meat-eaters.

However, if a vegetarian diet is poorly balanced or too strict, it may not provide enough of certain nutrients. The most widespread error committed by women who are new to vegetarianism is to incorrectly replace meat, chicken, and fish. If they merely replace them with cheese at every meal, they eat too much fat and not enough iron. If they eat only mountains of vegetables or whole grains, they are short of protein. Deficiency problems reported by scientists almost always involve young *strict vegetarian* women who are pregnant and their breast-fed babies or young children:

- Pregnant women who do not gain enough weight during pregnancy because of an incomplete diet will give birth to smaller babies and are more likely to experience complications in delivery.
- Some babies nursed by strict vegetarian mothers suffer from neurological problems caused by a lack of vitamin B_{12}. This deficiency *can* be fatal.
- Some young children raised in strict vegetarian families develop early signs of rickets, i.e. deformed leg and thorax bones, because of a lack of vitamin D in their diet.

Vegetarianism is beneficial as long as meals are well balanced and contain a wide range of complementary foods. The daily menu should contain:

- At least five servings of whole grain products.
- At least three servings of fruit.
- At least three servings of vegetables.
- At least one serving of tofu and legumes or the equivalent in soya milk.
- At least three servings of milk or dairy products.

The protein in grain is complemented by the protein in legumes and dairy products. Vegetarians who eat three meals a day that contain at least these recommended servings will be getting enough protein.

Strict vegetarians who do not eat dairy products should increase the servings of grain products and include some nuts or seeds to boost their calorie intake. They should also give priority to foods that are particularly high in iron and calcium to compensate for the lack of dairy and animal products (see pages 106 to 129).

When a vegetarian is pregnant or nursing, she should drink at least 500 mL (16 oz) of milk to obtain enough riboflavin, vitamin D, and vitamin B_{12}. The more varied her diet, the less likely she is to suffer from vitamin or mineral deficiencies.

Strict vegetarianism is not recommended during pregnancy or for children younger than two.

MACROBIOTICS

This eastern-inspired approach is part of an overall philosophy that dates back thousands of years. It is based on the principle of balance between *yin* (the quality of quiet, related to simplicity, receptiveness, femininity) and *yang* (creative action and masculinity). The macrobiotic diet is somewhat similar to a strict vegetarian diet. It was adapted for Westerners by George Oshawa, a Japanese philosopher who bridged the two cultures more than thirty years ago. His approach:

- Strives for a balance between *yin* and *yang*, vegetable and animal, cold and hot, fruit and grains.
- Includes several levels of menus ranging from a rather varied diet to a diet consisting exclusively of brown rice.
- Recommends eating locally produced organic vegetables only in season.
- Eliminates potatoes, tomatoes, and eggplant from the menu because they are considered too *yin*.
- Limits intake of liquids to 250 mL (1 cup) per day. (Water is *yin*; drinking too much of it affects the balance.) The "official" macrobiotic drink is *bancha* tea.
- Recommends slow and thorough chewing.
- Eliminates fruit in the event of illness.

Chewing well, eating more whole grains and locally grown organic vegetables and less sugar and fat will not harm anyone, but a strict application of Oshawa's principles does not always meet all nutrient requirements.

The fewer the foods permitted by the macrobiotic diet, the greater the risk of deficiency. Recently, there were reports of several serious cases of dietary deficiencies related to macrobiotics, including two deaths: teenagers who ate nothing but brown rice and drank small quantities of water. Other cases involved young children in the Boston area who did not drink milk and had no source of vitamin D. They suffered from the early stages of rickets and their growth, compared to other children of the same age, was retarded.

For this reason, a macrobiotic diet is not recommended for children younger than two and any excessively strict application should be avoided at any age.

THE ANTI-CANDIDA DIET

This diet, developed in 1983 in the United States by Dr. William Crook, is addressed to women suffering from *Candida albicans*, a disease associated with too much yeast in the digestive tract.

According to the promoters of this therapy, the problems caused by excess yeast range from chronic fatigue to intestinal bloating and repeated infections. These problems are connected with frequent administration of antibiotics, birth control pills, and too much sugar in the diet. To free the digestive tract of excess yeast and relieve the symptoms, the food strategy aims to starve the yeast. The menu, which is very strict:

- Eliminates all concentrated sugars: white sugar, honey, etc.
- Eliminates all alcohol: beer, wine, etc.
- Eliminates all fruit, including fresh fruit, fruit juice and dried fruit.
- Eliminates all dairy products except yogurt.
- Eliminates all products containing yeast, such as bread.
- Eliminates all foods that may contain mould: peanuts, fermented soya products (soya sauce, tempeh, tamari sauce), mushrooms, vinegar, tea, coffee, and herbal teas.
- Eliminates all canned foods.

The following products can be eaten as desired on this diet:

- Beef, poultry, fish, legumes, tofu.
- Cooked and raw vegetables (except potatoes, squash, and corn).
- Oil and butter.
- Nuts and seeds (except peanuts).
- Water.

The following can be eaten in moderation:

- Brown rice, barley, corn, oats, millet, and grain products containing no yeast.

This diet is not balanced: it is particularly low in calcium and is likely to result in a shortage of iron and vitamin B complex. With such a long list of forbidden foods, few people can manage to eat enough to function normally.

I have met a number of women who have followed this strict diet. They had all lost weight but their strength had been sapped. Furthermore, their symptoms had not always been completely relieved. It is possible to adapt this approach to produce fewer deficiencies. The American College of Allergists and Immunologists considers this treatment experimental.

IT'S UP TO YOU

There will always be new diets appearing on the scene. Some may look interesting, others will be frankly dangerous.

I suggest that you critically evaluate any unconventional diet and analyze it carefully before adopting or rejecting it. Common sense is always the best guide.

A good diet can:

- Eliminate refined products (white bread, bleached flour, white rice and pasta).
- Reduce concentrated sugars to a minimum (white sugar, brown sugar, honey, maple syrup).
- Reduce total fat intake (butter, margarine, oil, meat, cheese, fried foods).
- Increase the amount of dietary fiber (whole grains, fresh fruits and vegetables, nuts, legumes).
- Reduce the amount of salted and smoked foods.
- Discourage food additives.
- Recommend eating organically grown, additive-free foods.
- Recommend chewing food longer.
- Suggest moderate doses of vitamin and mineral supplements (see table on supplements, pp. 163 to 171).

BUT

- A diet should never eliminate an entire basic food category such as:
  All dairy products
  All fruits
  All meat, poultry, fish, legumes, or tofu

All nuts
All whole grains, all breads
All vegetables
- It should retain a good source of protein at each meal (milk, yogurt, cheese, tofu, grains, meat, fish, or poultry).
- It should not complicate your diet to the extent that it is impossible to eat with other people.
- It should not impose restrictions on the amount of water you can drink.
- It should not impose a rigid meal schedule.
- It should not eliminate nutritious snacks.

If the diet does not meet these conditions, look elsewhere!

SETTING NEW PRIORITIES

7

Less Fat!

Women have been the target of all diet-related messages in recent years. Submerged in a deluge of media hype about thinness, many have become victims of overly strict diets that have ruined their eating habits. Many have lost sight of the requirements of a proper healthy diet.

The return to a balanced diet proposed in this chapter embodies a kinder philosophy: gentle dietetics. The modifications suggested should create a harmonious context for good food. They do not involve the application of strict dietary rules.

This gentle approach creates new links with foods that are good to you. It encourages you to adopt a better eating style while giving your body and mind time to adjust. Think about it before acting; avoid abrupt changes that stress your whole being. This new eating strategy can even take a year or two to implement if necessary!

Women have little room for error, given their current nutritional deficiencies. Since they have never eaten so little, they must make wiser food choices! This approach emphasizes fresh, healthy foods that have undergone minimum transformation by the food industry. I present foods as investments and emphasize the investments that give the highest return: foods rich in calcium, magnesium, and iron. Foods loaded with sugar and refined fats are not on the list. The charts in the chapters which follow and in the appendix will help you plan menus to obtain the highest possible return. You will discover, for example, that:

- A glass of skim milk contains three and a half times more calcium than a scoop of ice cream.

- A banana contains eight times more vitamin B_6 than a bowl of strawberries.
- Pineapple is a better source of calcium, iron, and magnesium than peaches.
- Dried figs contain much more iron and calcium than other dried fruits.
- Bran cereal is an excellent source of magnesium and iron.
- Whole-wheat bread contains three times more magnesium and five times more vitamin B_6 than white bread.
- A serving of fresh trout contains more iron than any other fish.
- Oysters are absolutely loaded with zinc.
- Leafy green vegetables such as spinach and Swiss chard contain three times more magnesium and iron than other vegetables.
- Legumes are a major source of nutrients.
- Unhulled sesame seeds are exceptionally rich in iron and calcium.
- A small spoonful of dried thyme contains more iron than a lamb chop!

You will also discover some foods that are so rich in certain nutrients that I have rated them "best food investment" in their categories.

Here are some examples.

For Iron:

All kinds of liver, and oysters
Enriched Cream of Wheat, bran cereals
Legumes
Blackstrap molasses, dried figs

For Calcium:

Dairy products
Dark green leafy vegetables
Rhubarb
Dried figs
Canned fish eaten with their bones

For Magnesium:

Legumes and tofu
Bran cereals and wheat germ
Dark green leafy vegetables

For Zinc:

Fresh oysters
Liver
Crab and lobster
Wheat germ and bran cereal
Legumes

For Vitamin B$_6$:

Legumes
Liver
Potatoes and bananas
Certain types of fish

If women who consume only 1,500 to 1,700 calories per day want to satisfy their nutritional requirements, they have no choice but to concentrate on the best possible food investments. This is the only way they can meet their nutrition challenge!

This "good investment" strategy does not overlook eating pleasure either—in itself a great health booster! The strategy can work only if it combines good food choices with meals that are a pleasure to eat. An "improved menu plan" for healthy women (page 146) is also suggested. It takes into account the major obstacles in women's lives and does not systematically avoid ready-to-eat products or canned foods (see previous chapter). It sets four major priorities which automatically direct food choices toward the best investments.

FOUR MAJOR PRIORITIES

A balanced diet can be achieved only by first doing an inventory of what is missing in women's diets today:

• Not enough iron, calcium, magnesium, zinc.
• Not enough vitamin B$_6$.
• Not enough calories during pregnancy.
• Not enough protein in new vegetarians' diets.
• Not enough dietary fiber.
• Too much fat.

Rather than looking at each of these shortcomings separately and making a list of nine priorities, I propose four priorities that will cover all of these problems. These new priorities are:

1. Decrease total fat intake and choose better fats.
2. Increase intake of iron-rich foods and facilitate iron absorption.
3. Increase intake of calcium-rich foods and facilitate calcium absorption.
4. Increase intake of magnesium-rich foods and facilitate magnesium absorption.

If you readjust your intake of fat, iron, calcium, and magnesium, you will automatically be taking in enough zinc, vitamin B_6, fiber, and every other nutrient required for your well-being. The reason for this is very simple. When you incorporate the best sources of calcium, iron, and magnesium into your diet, you will find that they are the very best foods on the market and are rich in other nutrients as well.

This is a novel proposal—the result of countless calculations to prove that it really works! Let's say it again: if your diet is rich in calcium, iron, and magnesium, you will automatically meet all of your nutritional requirements!

These four priorities are implemented in the improved menu plan (pages 146 to 150), which should be adopted gradually. Before moving on to the menu plan, however, I would like to discuss each of the priorities more thoroughly.

DECREASE TOTAL FAT INTAKE AND CHOOSE BETTER FATS

Women currently take in about 40 per cent of their total calories in the form of fat! A few years ago, the war on fat was directed mainly against the "saturated" fats in meat, butter, and cheese because of their role in increasing blood cholesterol levels. Now, although no one disputes the relationship between high intake of saturated fats and increased levels of blood cholesterol, we also realize that saturated fat intake must be reduced, particularly by those who are the most vulnerable, i.e., postmenopausal women with a cholesterol level of more than 220 mg/dL and those with a family history of heart disease.

More recently, the war on fat has spread to all excess fat,

even including the best polyunsaturated fats. Why? Because research has revealed a possible link between high fat intake (any kind) and an increased risk of breast and intestinal cancer. As a result, the U.S. National Research Council as well as the Canadian Cancer Society and the Canadian Association of Dietitians all recommend reducing fat intake to less than 30 per cent of total daily calories. To reach this healthier level, calculations are based on what you are currently eating. For example, if you eat large quantities of food without gaining weight, you can eat more fat than someone who eats very little food, the objective always being to maintain fat at a proportion of 30 per cent of the total calorie intake for the day.

The daily acceptable quota for a woman is about 50 to 70 g of fat.

There is no need to weigh your food! Just take a close look at your regular menu. You should be able to guess at your normal fat intake by roughly calculating what you eat on a regular basis. The following list of foods should make this easier for you.

MEAT, FISH, POULTRY, AND ALTERNATIVES	QUANTITY	FAT (IN GRAMS)
Pork and beef sausage	90 g (3 oz)	32.5
Lamb chop (fat and lean)	90 g (3 oz)	32
Pork spareribs	3	27.5
Roast beef (rump: fat and lean)	90 g (3 oz)	20
Pork chop	90 g (3 oz)	19
Lean ground beef	90 g (3 oz)	18.5
Peanut butter	32 g (1 oz)	16
Egg fried in butter	1	14
Fried chicken	90 g (3 oz)	11.5
Veal	90 g (3 oz)	10
Lamb chop (lean only)	90 g (3 oz)	10
Pecans	14 g (1/2 oz)	10
Almonds	18 g (1/2 oz)	10
Head cheese	26 g (1 oz)	10
Side bacon	3 slices	10
Walnuts	12 g (1/2 oz)	8
Broiled salmon	90 g (3 oz)	6.7
Leg of lamb (lean only)	90 g (3 oz)	6.5

MEAT, FISH, POULTRY, AND ALTERNATIVES	QUANTITY	FAT (IN GRAMS)
Soybeans (cooked)	95 g (1/2 cup)	5
Tofu	120 g (4 oz)	5
Egg	1	5
Back bacon	2 slices	4
Chickpeas (cooked)	211 g (1 cup)	4
Roast turkey (white meat)	90 g (3 oz)	3.5
Chicken (white meat)	90 g (3 oz)	3
Fish, clams, crab, lobster, shrimp, scallops, oysters	90 g (3 oz)	2.5
Lentils (cooked)	211 g (1 cup)	1
Tuna (in water)	90 g (3 oz)	1
White beans (cooked)	137 g (1 cup)	trace

MILK AND DAIRY PRODUCTS		
Ice cream	140 g (1 cup)	16
Cheddar cheese	45 g (1 1/2 oz)	15
Colby cheese	45 g (1 1/2 oz)	15
Swiss cheese	45 g (1 1/2 oz)	15
Whole milk	250 mL (8 oz)	9
Mozzarella (part-skim) cheese	45 g (1 1/2 oz)	7.5
Skim milk yogurt	260 g (1 cup)	2.5
Skim milk processed cheese	45 g (1 1/2 oz)	2.5
Cottage cheese, skimmed	120 g (1/2 cup)	trace
1% milk	250 mL (1 cup)	trace

BREADS AND GRAIN PRODUCTS		
Cheesecake	1 piece	18
Danish pastry	1	17.6
Apple pie	1 piece	13.1
Croissant	1	12
Doughnut	1	11.2
Buttered popcorn	10 g (1 cup)	10
Cookies	4	9
Whole-wheat crackers	4	6
Bread with 1 pat butter	1 slice	5.7
Bran muffin, small	1	3.9
Cooked oatmeal	240 g (1 cup)	2.5
Barley	200 g (1 cup)	2.3
Millet (uncooked)	51 g (1/4 cup)	1.5
Brown rice (steamed)	200 g (1 cup)	1.2
Melba toast	4	0.8
Whole-wheat bread	1 slice	0.7
Pumpernickel bread	1 slice	0.4
Unbuttered popcorn	6 g (1 cup)	trace
Whole-wheat pasta	148 g (5 oz)	trace
Bagel (plain, onion, poppy or sesame seed)	1	trace

Quick References	Fat Content
90 g (3 oz) meat (beef, pork, lamb)	15 g
90 g (3 oz) poultry, fish, game	8 g
14 g (1 tbsp) butter or margarine	12 g
15 mL (1 tbsp) oil	14 g
500 mL (2 cups) whole milk	18 g
500 mL (2 cups) 2% milk	10 g
500 mL (2 cups) skim milk	0 g
60 g (2 oz) cheese	18 g
12 g (2 tbsp) nuts, sunflower, or sesame seeds	10 g
1 slice whole-wheat bread	1 g
195 g (1 cup) lentils or chickpeas, cooked	3 g
195 g (1 cup) soybeans, cooked	11 g
Fresh fruit	0 g
Avocado half	18 g
Fresh or frozen vegetables	0 g
50 g French fries (10)	8 g

A rather sedentary adult woman who consumes between 1,500 and 1,700 calories per day should limit her intake to approximately 50 to 55 g of fat per day.

On the other hand, *a dieting woman* who eats very little needs far less than 50 g of fat per day.

A teenager, who has a healthy appetite and eats more than her mother, can allow herself at least 60 g of fat per day.

An athlete or a very active woman who uses up a great deal of energy and eats enormous portions without gaining weight can eat more than 65 g of fat per day.

A pregnant woman or a nursing mother who must eat more than ever to meet all her needs (more than 2,200 calories per day is recommended) can consume at least 70 g of fat per day.

Reaching these acceptable limits does not mean eliminating meat or dairy products from the menu. However, by making the best food investments, you can easily choose foods with the least amount of fat in each food group (see tables above). For example, you can opt for:

• Fresh lean meat rather than processed meats and bacon.
• Cheese with the lowest fat content (see table below).
• Steaming, baking, or broiling instead of frying in butter and oil.

- Plain fresh or frozen fish instead of fish that has been breaded or served in rich sauce.
- Bread instead of cookies.
- Fruit instead of pastry for dessert.

Low-Fat Cheeses: Butterfat Content

FRESH CHEESE	
Cottage	0.08%-4%
Ricotta	10%-13%

SOFT REFINED CHEESES	
Brie, Camembert	15%-20%

PROCESSED CHEESES	
Skim-milk cheese (wedge)	6%
Slices	7%

CHEESE SPREADS	
Light	16.5%
Regular, processed	20%

FRESH GOAT CHEESE	
Regular or flavored	14%-20%

SOFT UNREFINED CHEESES	
Regular or flavored	15%-20%
Bocconcini	20%

SEMI-FIRM CHEESES	
Skim-milk, part skim-milk cheese	4%-7%
Part-skim mozzarella	15%
Regular mozzarella, cacciotta	20%

There are other easy ways to limit your fat intake:

- Bread eaten without butter saves 4 g fat for every pat of butter or margarine you eliminate.

- A poached egg instead of a fried egg saves 8 g fat.
- 125 g (1/2 cup) skim milk yogurt instead of ice cream saves 10 g fat.
- 6 g (1 cup) plain popcorn instead of ten potato chips eliminates 7 g fat.
- A bran muffin instead of an apple turnover cuts out 10 g fat.
- A bagel instead of a doughnut eliminates 9 g fat.
- A crusty roll instead of a Danish pastry saves 13 g fat.
- A baked potato instead of French fries eliminates 16 g fat.
- A 90-g (3-oz) steak instead of a 240-g (8-oz) steak will save you 15 g fat.

WHICH FAT TO CHOOSE?

Choosing the best fat to use is much more complicated than deciding between margarine and butter. The only fats required for good health are those that contain essential fatty acids. These are called "essential" because the body is unable to produce them itself and must obtain them from food. They play a crucial role in tissue growth, cell membrane permeability and the maintenance of healthy skin.

Here are a few basic principles to help you choose the fat that is the best investment.

The Less Refined the Better

Cold-pressed *polyunsaturated oils* (corn, sunflower, linseed, safflower) are, in principle, unrefined oils.[1] Although they do not contain any more essential fatty acids than regular polyunsaturated oil sold in the supermarket, they do contain more vitamin E, a natural antioxidant. They keep well in the refrigerator and are the best investments of all the polyunsaturated oils.

The *polyunsaturated oils* (corn, sunflower, linseed, saf-

---

[1] Some oils sold in natural food stores say "cold-pressed" on the label. There is no guarantee, however, that these oils are unrefined. The more an oil is processed, the more its nutritive value is affected. The hydrogenation of vegetable oil has revolutionized the fat market, but in addition to making vegetable oils less vulnerable to rancidity, it has reduced their essential fatty acid content.

flower) sold in the supermarket contain just as much essential fatty acid as the cold-pressed oils. They are a good food investment, but have lost some vitamin E.

A *partly hydrogenated vegetable oil* has lost some of its essential fatty acids in the hydrogenation process. Read the labels carefully and avoid partly hydrogenated oils.

Butter, a largely "saturated" fat, is not highly processed. It remains a good food investment as long as it is eaten in small quantities by women who are not at high risk (less than 220 mg/dL of blood cholesterol and no family history of cardiovascular disease).

Hydrogenated vegetable fat used in piecrusts, cakes, crackers, chips, and cookies has no nutritional benefits because most of the essential fatty acids have been eliminated by hydrogenation.

Margarine made with hydrogenated vegetable oil (indicated on the label) is not a good food investment since it has been highly processed and has lost its beneficial qualities.

Margarine made with non-hydrogenated corn or sunflower oil (indicated on the label) is a good investment for women who are vulnerable to cardiovascular disease. It is, however, only one dietary measure among others to take in reducing blood cholesterol levels.

Virgin or first-press olive oil is a good food investment.

Since the early 1960s, top marks have invariably been given to the polyunsaturated oils: corn, sunflower, safflower, soya, and linseed. Recent research has reversed this trend, however, and now recognizes the benefits of olive oil. The extraction of this mono-unsaturated oil requires very little processing. Olive oil has been a staple of the Mediterranean countries for centuries and apparently has a protective effect on the cardiovascular system.

Omega 3 fatty acids in fish are also recommended.

Fats found in fish products are not processed by the body in the same way as those derived from other sources. These fatty acids are polyunsaturated but take the form of "omega 3" instead of "omega 6", which is the form of all oils originating from vegetable matter *except* linseed oil.[1]

Omega 3 fatty acids have been studied by a number of teams of scientists. Results show that they seem to provide protection against strokes by slowing down blood coagulation and contributing to a drop in triglyceride levels in the blood. They also seem to have an anti-carcinogenic effect and can act as an anti-inflammatory agent in certain cases of rheumatoid arthritis.

To benefit from all this, there's no need to replace your salad oil with cod liver oil! Just increase your regular intake of fatty fish like salmon, mackerel, sardines, and trout. Two or three fish or seafood meals a week are an excellent food investment at any age.

To summarize, in order to decrease your total fat intake and choose the best fats:

- Use a moderate amount of different top-quality fats (make the best possible investments).
- Choose foods with the least amount of fat (see tables on pp. 99 to 101).
- Cook with as little fat as possible.
- Alternate between a polyunsaturated oil (corn, sunflower) and a mono-unsaturated oil (olive).
- Eat fatty fish regularly.
- Limit your total intake of visible fat (oil, margarine, butter) to 25 g (2 tbsp) of fat per day and always include a minimum of 15 mL (1 tbsp) polyunsaturated fat.
- Respect your daily fat-intake limit as mentioned earlier.

If you don't always get your daily quota of fat, don't worry! As long as you use 1 tbsp of polyunsaturated oil per day, you'll meet your essential fatty acid requirements. And remember not to exceed 50 g of fat daily unless you are in one of the special categories mentioned on page 101.

---

[1] Linseed oil, despite the omega 3 fatty acids it contains, does not have all the same properties as fish oils.

8

More Iron!

INCREASE INTAKE OF
IRON-RICH FOODS AND
FACILITATE IRON ABSORPTION.

One woman in five has exhausted her iron stores and one in ten is actually anemic. Only three women in five today are meeting their bodies' iron requirements.

This is the most widespread nutritional deficiency facing women. And it affects all women, from teenagers to seniors, all over the world.

Easy to Explain

Women are affected by iron shortages because they lose iron in their menstrual blood each month and are unable to make up the deficit in the foods they eat. Often, they eat too little and do not invest in the right foods. Considering their current food choices, they would have to eat twice as much to meet their needs. Better nutrition remains the challenge!

Many women suffer from iron deficiency but never complain. Yet iron-poor blood contains less hemoglobin and transports oxygen less efficiently from the lungs to the tissues. The immune system suffers a partial breakdown and the enzymes that help transform calories into energy do not work properly. Result: these women feel tired and are more prone to infection. They are often exhausted, short of breath, and barely able to make it to the end of the day.

Needs Change Over the Life Cycle

First, refer to the table at the end of this section.

Women need a great deal of iron throughout their reproductive years, from puberty to menopause. Once menstruation ends, iron requirements decrease but women who take hormone therapy still need iron for a few years after menopause.

Starting at puberty, *teenage girls* must increase their iron intake. Unfortunately, nutrition surveys show that two out of five young girls are seriously short of iron.

Adult women need forty per cent more iron than men of their generation; this difference between the sexes persists until, and sometimes after, menopause. Insufficient iron intake is often related to overconsumption of refined, sweetened foods.

Vegetarian women have the same iron requirements as their meat-eating sisters. Although their diet does not include red meat, recent studies show that they do not experience more iron deficiency than non-vegetarians. On the other hand, many women who are newly converted to vegetarianism tend to replace meat with cheese or other dairy products that are low in iron. They are the ones who are likely to suffer from iron deficiency.

Older women who are no longer menstruating do not need as much iron. However, they must still pay attention to their choice of foods because they eat less and are thus more vulnerable to deficiencies.

During pregnancy, the volume of the mother's blood increases, the placenta is formed, and the fetus develops its own iron requirements. This is the time when the mother's needs peak. Recommendations vary depending on the country, but all are high, about 1,000 mg per pregnancy. To meet these requirements, pregnant women must adjust their food intake and generally take iron supplements (see appendix).

Nursing mothers secrete a small amount of iron in their milk that is very well assimilated by the baby until the age of four months. This iron is even better for babies than the iron that is added to formula! For this reason, nursing mothers need to step up their iron intake, although not as much as during pregnancy. Supplements are often recommended for nursing mothers to help them meet their own needs and rebuild their reserves.

After giving blood (400–500 mL), women lose the equivalent of 200 mg of iron. They must adjust their menu accordingly to restore the proper concentration of iron in their hemoglobin. It is recommended that 0.5 mg of iron be added *each day over a year* to compensate for the blood donation.

Women who use an IUD for birth control bleed much more than women who take the pill. They must therefore watch their intake of iron-rich food very carefully.

When they are in training, women *athletes'* iron requirements increase. Some researchers recommend iron supplements and all favor a generous amount of iron in the diet.

Iron

AGE	ACTUAL INTAKE*	RECOMMENDED INTAKE**	
		CANADA (1983)	U.S.A. (1980)
13-15		13 mg	18 mg
16-18		14 mg	18 mg
19-24	10.5 mg	14 mg	18 mg
25-49		14 mg	18 mg
50-74		7 mg	10 mg
75+		7 mg	10 mg
Pregnancy	13.2 mg	20 mg	30-60 mg supplement
Lactation	13.3 mg	15 mg	30-60 mg supplement for 2-3 months post partum.

* Figures taken from research cited in references in Chapter 1.

** The recommended allowances or nutrient intakes vary from country to country. These figures reflect the philosophy of one group of experts and may not correspond with those of another group. They are revised and updated periodically, based on the most current scientific research.

The Art of Eating Enough Iron

The challenge can be met! If you want your iron intake to reach the amounts recommended for your particular situation, all you have to do is focus on foods that are rich in this mineral. Official recommendations are:

• 14 to 18 mg per day from puberty to menopause
• 20 mg per day for pregnant women
• 15 to 20 mg per day for nursing mothers

If you like being precise, you can check all the sources of iron by consulting the lists on the following pages. On the other hand, if you prefer to simplify things, you can draw up a menu from the categories below, which represent averages for each food group:

- One serving of whole-grain products provides 1.4 mg of iron.
- One serving of fruit provides 0.5 mg of iron.
- One serving of vegetables provides 1.2 mg of iron.
- One serving of meat, poultry, or fish provides 1.8 mg of iron.
- One serving of legumes provides 4.7 mg of iron.
- One serving of dairy products provides 0.15 mg of iron.

These figures give an indication of how your menu can be oriented. Don't forget to concentrate on the best food investments, i.e., foods that exceed the food group average. "Exceptional" iron investments contain two or three times more iron than other foods. Some foods can be included in your menu every day (*). Others should be eaten only once a week.

* • 40 g (3/4 cup) enriched cereal provides 5.6 mg of iron.
* • 45 g (1/2 cup) bran cereal provides 6 mg of iron.
  • 90 g (3 oz) liver provides 12 mg of iron.
* • 85 g (1/2 cup) enriched cooked Cream of Wheat provides 8 mg of iron.
  • 90 g (1 cup) cooked spinach provides 6.8 mg of iron.
  • 90 g (3 oz) fresh oysters provides 5 mg of iron.
* • 60 ml (1/4 cup) of enriched infant cereal provides 3.3 mg of iron.
* • 15 ml (1 tbsp) of blackstrap molasses provides 3.2 mg of iron.

Women who manage to consume enough iron are those who eat a lot of fruit, vegetables, and grain products and avoid sweetened beverages, fried foods, and pastries.

The "improved menu plan" suggested in the concluding chapter follows these lines. It suggests a certain number of servings for each food group that will meet not only iron requirements but also women's three other major food priorities.

Facilitate Iron Absorption

Not only is it important to eat the right amount of iron, you must also ensure that it is properly absorbed. Since iron shortages are so prevalent and do so much harm, many studies have been done on how to increase its absorption by the body. We now know which factors are beneficial and which are detrimental to iron absorption.

Factors that Facilitate Iron Absorption

- Iron is absorbed two or three times more efficiently when taken with foods high in vitamin C. Researchers have established the figure of 75 mg of vitamin C per meal, which is a relatively easy amount to find in fruits and vegetables. Incorporating 75 mg of vitamin C into each meal is the best way to enhance iron absorption (see tables on pages 112 and 113).
- Animal products—meat, poultry, or fish—enhance iron absorption. A minimum of 30 g (1 oz) per meal is enough to improve the iron absorption process. For example, the iron contained in brown rice pilaf with vegetables is absorbed better if a small amount of chicken or seafood is added to the dish.
- Wine, in moderate amounts, also seems to aid iron absorption.

Factors that Inhibit Iron Absorption

- Tea is iron's worst enemy. The tannins in tea combine with the iron and block its absorption. Coffee also plays a negative role, but it is not nearly as bad as tea.
- Calcium supplements and antacids with a calcium carbonate base inhibit iron absorption when taken at the same time as iron-rich foods or an iron supplement. They can, however, be taken between meals, at bedtime, or in the form of a multi-vitamin tablet containing vitamin C. Dietary fiber does not inhibit iron absorption. Research has indicated that when adequate amounts of iron are consumed, the body soon adapts to an intake of about 25 to 30 g of fiber per day.

COOKING WITH IRON

A weekly serving of liver or another organ meat is like taking an iron supplement! Unfortunately, liver is not usually very popular. If you like liver and are looking for new ideas (and especially if you *don't* but are willing to experiment!) here's one of my favorite recipes:

CHINESE-STYLE LIVER

Makes 4 servings
Preparation time: less than 3 minutes
Cooking time: maximum 8 minutes

500 g (1 lb) very fresh liver, sliced thin
2 to 3 tbsp tamari sauce (natural soya sauce)
3 tbsp freshly squeezed lemon juice
1 clove garlic, pressed through a garlic press
Fresh chives or parsley, chopped

Prepare the marinade by combining tamari sauce, lemon juice, garlic and chives.

Place the slices of liver in an ovenproof dish and cover with marinade. Let stand 5 to 10 minutes if possible.

Broil liver in the marinade 6 inches from heat for 4 to 5 minutes, turn and cook the other side for 3 more minutes.

Serve immediately with fresh pasta, brown rice, or millet.

This dish can also be made in a wok if you like. Cut the liver into thin strips and sauté in the marinade for a few minutes over high heat.

A Little More Iron Here and There

• Eat dried figs instead of other dried fruit.
• Add some prune juice to mixed fruit juice or jellied fruit dishes.
• Sprinkle chopped nuts over your yogurt, cereal, or fruit compote.
• Add enriched infant cereal to the flour when baking muffins or fruit breads. Sprinkle some in vegetable soup before serving.
• Replace the jam on your toast with figs puréed with orange zest.
• Be generous with thyme in your soups, quiches, and vinaigrettes.
• Sprinkle applesauce, yogurt, and milkshakes with cinnamon.
• Don't forget that mushrooms are relatively high in iron.

- Use lentils "incognito" in spaghetti sauce, shepherd's pie, and lasagna.
- Make a well-seasoned lentil soup and serve it sprinkled with lots of minced fresh parsley for color.

To obtain at least 75 mg of vitamin C* per meal, and aid iron absorption . . .

Choose one of the *fruits* or *a combination of fruits* from the following list:

Frozen orange juice, diluted	1 large glass
Orange juice, freshly squeezed	1 large glass
Frozen grapefruit juice, diluted	1 large glass
Grapefruit juice, freshly squeezed	1 large glass
Grape juice, vitamin C added	1 large glass
Canned pineapple juice, vitamin C added	1 large glass
Apple juice, vitamin C added	1 large glass
Canned apricot nectar, vitamin C added	1 large glass
Papaya, fresh	half
Strawberries, fresh	150 g (1 cup)
Cantaloupe, fresh	half
Orange, fresh	1 medium
Kiwi	2 small
Mango	half
+ strawberries, fresh or frozen	75 g (1/2 cup)
Cantaloupe	quarter
+ strawberries, fresh or frozen	60 g (1/2 cup)

OR

Choose one of the *vegetables* or *a combination of vegetables* from this list:

Broccoli, raw	1 stalk
Broccoli, cooked	170 g (1 cup)
Brussels sprouts, cooked	7–8 medium
Cauliflower, raw	100 g (1 cup)
Cauliflower, cooked	200 g (1 cup)
Snow peas, cooked	170 g (1 cup)
Green pepper, raw	50–70 g (1)
Broccoli, cooked	80 g (1/2 cup)
+ sweet potato	160 g (1/2 cup)
Snow peas, cooked	85 g (1/2 cup)
+ red pepper	45 g (1/2 cup)
Vegetable juice	250 mL (1 cup)
+ cabbage salad	65 g (1/2 cup)

OR

Choose a *combination of fruits and vegetables* for the same meal:

Asparagus, cooked	4 spears
+ kiwi	2 small
Turnip, cooked	180 g (1 cup)
+ watermelon	1 slice
Potato, baked	1 medium

To obtain at least 75 mg of vitamin C* per meal, and aid iron absorption . . .

+ orange	1 medium
Red cabbage, grated, raw	75 g (1 cup)
+ honeydew melon	1 slice
Green beans, cooked	130 g (1 cup)
+ fresh strawberries	150 g (1 cup)
Sweet potato	340 g (1 cup)
+ fresh pineapple	165 g (1 cup)

Ref.: Nutrients in Canadian Foods, Health and Welfare Canada, Ottawa, 1987.

Nutrient Tables: Iron

The following charts provide comprehensive information on the iron content of the major food categories: bread and cereals, fruit, vegetables, meat, fish and poultry, legumes, milk and milk products, nuts and seeds, spices and herbs. Among all the foods listed, some are labeled "best food investments" because of their exceptional iron content in comparison with others of the same group.

These figures set the record straight but do not impose the use of a calculator every time you do your shopping list! You can easily improve your iron intake just by choosing more often those foods that are nearer the top of the list.

BREAD AND CEREALS	QUANTITY	IRON (mg)
Cream of Wheat, enriched, cooked*	121 g (1/2 cup)	8
Bran cereal (All Bran)*	35 g (1/2 cup)	6
Shreddies*	43 g (3/4 cup)	5.9
Raisin Bran*	42 g (3/4 cup)	5.6
Bran flakes*	40 g (3/4 cup)	5.3
Millet, dry	51 g (1/4 cup)	3.9
Wheat germ	30 g (1/4 cup)	3.6
Pasta, whole-wheat, uncooked	100 g (3 1/2 oz)	3
Macaroni, enriched, cooked	148 g (1 cup)	2.2
Baby cereal, enriched	5 g (2 tbsp)	1.7
Bagel	50 g (1)	1.6
Egg noodles, enriched, cooked	169 g (1 cup)	1.5
Bran muffin	40 g (1 medium)	1.4
Pumpernickel bread	32 g (1 slice)	0.8
Oat flakes, cooked	123 g (1/2 cup)	0.8
Shredded Wheat	25 g (1 biscuit)	0.8
Whole-wheat bread	28 g (1 slice)	0.8
White bread, enriched	24 g (1 slice)	0.7
Rye bread	25 g (1 slice)	0.7
Wheat bran	4.2 g (1 tbsp)	0.6
Pearl barley, cooked	105 g (1/2 cup)	0.6
White rice, enriched, cooked	92 g (1 cup)	0.6

BREAD AND CEREALS	QUANTITY	IRON (mg)
Brown rice, cooked	206 g (1 cup)	0.4
Red River cereal, cooked	125 g (1/2 cup)	0.4
Cream of Wheat, not enriched, cooked	121 g (1/2 cup)	0.3

Best food investment

FRUIT	QUANTITY	IRON (mg)
Prune juice, bottled*	250 mL (1 cup)	3.2
Figs, dried*	95 (5)	2.1
Raisins*	76 g (1/2 cup)	1.8
Prunes, dried	40 g (5)	1.0
Avocado	173 g (1/2)	1.0
Apple juice	250 mL (1 cup)	1.0
Dates, dried	80 g (10)	1.0
Blackberries	152 g (1 cup)	0.8
Pineapple, canned	164 g (1 cup)	0.7
Grape juice, bottled	250 mL (1 cup)	0.6
Apricots, fresh	105 g (3)	0.6
Cantaloupe	267 g (1/2)	0.6
Strawberries, fresh or frozen	157 g (1 cup)	0.6
Cherries, fresh	109 g (1 cup)	0.5
Grapefruit juice, bottled	205 mL (1 cup)	0.5
Banana	115 g (1 medium)	0.4
Kiwi	76 g (1 large)	0.4
Orange juice, frozen, diluted	250 mL (1 cup)	0.3
Watermelon, cubed	169 g (1 cup)	0.3
Rhubarb, cooked, sweetened	127 g (1/2 cup)	0.2
Blueberries	153 g (1 cup)	0.2
Nectarine	136 g (1)	0.2
Mango	207 g (1 medium)	0.2
Apple	138 g (1 medium)	0.2
Grapefruit	118 g (1/2)	0.1
Orange	131 g (1)	0.1
Peach	87 g (1)	0.1
Plum, fresh	66 g (1)	trace

Best food investment

VEGETABLES	QUANTITY	IRON (mg)
Spinach, cooked*	190 g (1 cup)	6.8
Swiss chard, cooked*	185 g (1 cup)	4
Beet greens, cooked	145 g (1 cup)	2.9
Potato, baked, with skin	206 g (1 medium)	2.7
Mushrooms, raw	74 g (1 cup)	2.7
Green peas, cooked	169 g (1 cup)	2.5
Tomatoes, cooked, canned	254 g (1 cup)	2

VEGETABLES	QUANTITY	IRON (mg)
Brussels sprouts, cooked	165 g (1 cup)	2
Broccoli, cooked	164 g (1 cup)	1.9
Sweet potato, cooked	144 g (1 cup)	1.9
Dandelion greens, cooked	105 g (1 cup)	1.9
Dandelion greens, raw	60 g (1 cup)	1.7
Green beans, cooked	132 g (1 cup)	1.7
Spinach, raw	59 g (1 cup)	1.6
Corn, frozen, cooked	173 g (1 cup)	1.5
Mushrooms, cooked	41 g (1/2 cup)	1.4
Leek, cooked	124 g (1 spear)	1.3
Broccoli, raw	151 g (1 spear)	1.3
Beet greens, raw	60 g (1 cup)	1.2
Kale, cooked	110 g (1 cup)	1.2
Beets, cooked	180 g (1 cup)	1.1
Parsnips, cooked	165 g (1 cup)	1
Carrots, cooked	165 g (1 cup)	1
Mustard greens, cooked	140 g (1 cup)	1
Green pepper, raw	73 g (1 medium)	0.9
Lettuce, leaf, raw	59 g (1 cup)	0.8
Mustard greens, raw	60 g (1 cup)	0.8
Turnip, cooked	165 g (1 cup)	0.8
Asparagus, cooked	120 g (8 spears)	0.8
Collards, cooked	145 g (1 cup)	0.8
Cauliflower, cooked	190 g (1 cup)	0.7
Okra, cooked	84 g (1/2 cup)	0.7
Zucchini, raw	190 g (1 cup)	0.7
Winter squash, cooked	217 g (1 cup)	0.6
Swiss chard, raw	38 g (1 cup)	0.6
Summer squash, cooked	190 g (1 cup)	0.6
Cauliflower, raw	106 g (1 cup)	0.6
Tomato, raw	123 g (1 medium)	0.6
Red cabbage, shredded, raw	74 g (1 cup)	0.5
Cabbage, shredded, raw	74 g (1 cup)	0.4
Carrot, raw	72 g (1 medium)	0.4
Eggplant, cooked	101 g (1 cup)	0.4
Endive, raw	50 g (1 cup)	0.2

* Best food investment

MEAT, FISH, POULTRY	QUANTITY	IRON (mg)
Pork liver, cooked*	90 g (3 oz)	18
Calves' liver, cooked*	90 g (3 oz)	13
Beef liver, cooked*	90 g (3 oz)	8
Chicken liver, cooked*	90 g (3 oz)	7.7
Oysters, raw	90 g (6 medium)	5
Trout, broiled	90 g (3 oz)	4.5
Clams, canned	90 g (3 oz)	3.6

MEAT, FISH, POULTRY	QUANTITY	IRON (mg)
Scallops, cooked	91 g (7)	3
Veal roast, cooked	90 g (3 oz)	3
Sardines, canned, with bones	90 g (3 oz)	2.6
Pork roast, cooked	90 g (3 oz)	2.6
Beef, lean, cooked	90 g (3 oz)	2.2
Herring, canned	90 g (3 oz)	1.6
Shrimp, canned	90 g (3 oz)	1.6
Lamb chop, lean, cooked	90 g (3 oz)	1.5
Chicken, without skin, cooked	90 g (3 oz)	1.5
Egg, cooked	50 g (1)	1.1
Haddock, raw	90 g (3 oz)	1
Cod, broiled	90 g (3 oz)	0.9
Salmon, canned, with bones	90 g (3 oz)	0.8
Lobster, canned	90 g (3 oz)	0.7
Crab, canned	90 g (3 oz)	0.7
Halibut, broiled	90 g (3 oz)	0.7
Ham, lean, cooked	90 g (3 oz)	0.7
Boston bluefish, broiled	90 g (3 oz)	0.6
Sole, cooked	90 g (3 oz)	0.4
Tuna, canned	90 g (3 oz)	0.2

* Best food investment

LEGUMES	QUANTITY	IRON (mg)
Black beans, cooked	200 g (1 cup)	7.9
Pinto beans, cooked	95 g (1 cup)	6.1
White kidney beans, cooked	137 g (1 cup)	5.4
Chickpeas, cooked	211 g (1 cup)	5.2
Soybeans, cooked	190 g (1 cup)	5.1
Red kidney beans, cooked	195 g (1 cup)	4.9
Lima beans, cooked	180 g (1 cup)	4.7
Lentils, cooked	211 g (1 cup)	4.4
Split peas, cooked	211 g (1 cup)	3.6
Lima beans, frozen, cooked	201 g (1 cup)	3.4
Black-eyed peas, cooked	264 g (1 cup)	3.3
Tofu	120 g (4 oz)	2.3

MILK AND MILK PRODUCTS	QUANTITY	IRON (mg)
Ricotta	130 g (1/2 cup)	0.5
Gruyère	30 g (1 oz)	0.3
Colby	30 g (1 oz)	0.2
Cheddar	30 g (1 oz)	0.2
Feta	30 g (1 oz)	0.2
Cottage cheese (2%)	120 g (1/2 cup)	0.2
Roquefort	30 g (1 oz)	0.1
Provolone	30 g (1 oz)	0.1
Brie	30 g (1 oz)	0.1

MILK AND MILK PRODUCTS	QUANTITY	IRON (mg)
Blue	30 g (1 oz)	0.1
Edam	30 g (1 oz)	0.1
Brick	30 g (1 oz)	0.1
Sliced cheese (processed)	30 g (1 oz)	0.1
Skim milk	250 mL (1 cup)	0.1
2% milk	250 mL (1 cup)	0.1
Whole milk	250 mL (1 cup)	0.1
Buttermilk	250 mL (1 cup)	0.1
Yogurt, plain	129 g (1/2 cup)	0.1
Ice cream, vanilla	70 g (1/2 cup)	0.1
Camembert	30 g (1 oz)	0.1
Gouda	30 g (1 oz)	0.1
Mozzarella, partially skimmed	30 g (1 oz)	0.1
Mozzarella	30 g (1 oz)	0.1
Swiss cheese	30 g (1 oz)	0.1
Skim milk powder	8 g (2 tbsp)	trace

NUTS AND SEEDS	QUANTITY	IRON (mg)
Cashews	14 large	1.7
Sesame seeds, whole, dried	9.5 g (1 tbsp)	1.3
Sunflower seeds, dried	18 g (2 tbsp)	1.1
Pistachios	30	1.1
Pecans	16	1.0
Sesame butter, stone ground	14 g (1 tbsp)	0.9
Almonds	15	0.7
Brazil nuts	4 large	0.6
Hazelnuts (filberts)	10	0.5
Coconut, sweetened, dried	25 g (1/4 cup)	0.3
Walnuts	5 halves	0.3
Peanut butter	16 g (1 tbsp)	0.3

SPICES AND HERBS	QUANTITY	IRON (mg)
Thyme	5 mL (1 tsp)	1.7
Cumin seed	5 mL (1 tsp)	1.4
Celery seed	5 mL (1 tsp)	0.9
Cinnamon	5 mL (1 tsp)	0.9
Oregano	5 mL (1 tsp)	0.6
Basil	5 mL (1 tsp)	0.6
Savory	5 mL (1 tsp)	0.5
Fennel seed	5 mL (1 tsp)	0.4
Dill seed	5 mL (1 tsp)	0.3
Poppy seed	5 mL (1 tsp)	0.2
Cloves, ground	5 mL (1 tsp)	0.2
Allspice	5 mL (1 tsp)	0.1

9

More Calcium!

INCREASE INTAKE OF CALCIUM-RICH FOODS AND FACILITATE CALCIUM ABSORPTION

Many women who don't eat enough high-calcium foods right from childhood accumulate a huge deficit over the years. Fortunately, it's never too late to turn the situation around!

Deficiencies Can Have Serious Consequences

Until the early 1980s, calcium was considered an insignificant part of a woman's diet and not much was heard about it. The alarm sounded when the cost to repair the damage caused by calcium deficiencies began to exceed health-care budgets.

In North America, one woman in four suffers from *osteoporosis*, a bone disease that decreases bone mass and makes the victim more susceptible to fractures. The problem particularly affects thin white women with a small bone structure who are not very active physically. Women whose mothers seem to have "shrunk" a few inches are particularly vulnerable.

A lack of calcium is not the only factor responsible for this condition, but it plays an important role.

Needs Change Over the Life Cycle

First, refer to the table at the end of this section.

Teenage girls need more calcium than adult women. Starting at age ten, they must prepare themselves for a major growth spurt, in which their bones grow quickly and increase in mass. Bone mass reaches its peak by age thirty. *A pregnant or nursing teenager* has even greater needs and must add the amount of calcium required for her pregnancy to her normal requirements. Adequate calcium intake can protect her bone mass. A combined calcium and vitamin D supplement may be beneficial.

Adult women continue to build bone mass and strengthen the skeleton until about age thirty. Their level of physical activity as well as what they eat and drink play a decisive role in determining their bone capital. After age thirty, they must try to protect this capital by keeping calcium loss to a minimum.

Pregnant women have greater needs right from the onset of pregnancy. All of the calcium stored in their bones in the first months will be transferred to the fetus in the final months of pregnancy.

Nursing mothers supply the baby with 200 to 350 mg of calcium per day in their milk. They can damage their own bones if they neglect their calcium intake during this critical period.

At the onset of menopause, women experience an abrupt loss of female hormones, which leads to decreased calcium absorption and increases the rate of bone loss. That is why calcium needs increase at about age fifty. Women absolutely *must compensate* for this accelerated loss. Unfortunately, research confirms that the message is still not getting through. Today's older women *still* take in less and less calcium.

Elderly women consume very little calcium and are unable to absorb it very effectively. Regular physical activity and exposure to sunlight can be beneficial. Adequate calcium intake is essential.

Strict vegetarians who do not drink milk or eat cheese or yogurt must do some nutritional acrobatics to find the calcium they need in fruits and vegetables. This is a major challenge! A calcium and vitamin D supplement may be necessary, especially during pregnancy and nursing, and after menopause.

Women who are bedridden lose 200 to 300 mg of calcium per day because the skeleton is immobilized. Only a return to normal activities, or at least maintaining an upright position for a few hours a day can help restore bone mineralization.

Women who are lactose-intolerant, who have trouble digesting milk and have cramps or diarrhea after eating dairy products seem to absorb calcium as well as anyone else, despite their discomfort. These women should assess the amount of dairy products they can tolerate without problems. Once they determine their tolerance level, they have two choices:

- Add Lactaid, a commercial enzyme available in pharmacies, to liquid milk, or swallow an enzyme tablet after eating cheese or yogurt (this enzyme, sold in drop or tablet form, digests the lactose and reduces or eliminates discomfort in most cases).
- Forget about dairy products and compensate by regularly eating other high-calcium foods (tables on pages 125 to 129) or by taking calcium supplements.

Calcium

AGE	ACTUAL INTAKE*	RECOMMENDED INTAKE**	
		CANADA (1983)	U.S.A. (1980)
10-12	720-800 mg	1000 mg	800-1200 mg
13-15		800 mg	1200 mg
16-18		700 mg	1200 mg
19-24	500-700 mg	700 mg	800 mg
25-49		700 mg	800 mg
50-74	490-800 mg	800 mg	800 mg
75+	500 mg	800 mg	800 mg
Pregnancy	760-1500 mg	1200 mg	1200 mg
Lactation	1060 mg (1500 mg with supplement)	1200 mg	1200 mg

* Figures taken from research cited in references in Chapter 1.

** The recommended allowances or nutrient intakes vary from country to country. These figures reflect the philosophy of one group of experts and may not correspond with those of another group.
They are revised and updated periodically, based on the most current scientific research.

Where to Find the Necessary Calcium

This challenge can also be met, since calcium is just about everywhere! Calcium is present naturally in many foods and is added to others. And new types of supplements appear on the market each day.

Suggested daily calcium intake is

- At least 800 mg of calcium from adolescence to age thirty.
- At least 1,000 mg of calcium after age thirty.
- At least 1,200 mg of calcium for pregnant women or nursing mothers.

Some experts recommend as much as 1,500 mg per day for post-menopausal women and studies are now being done on the impact of such dosages. Some recent studies have cast doubt on the real benefits of so much calcium. Doses as high as 2,000 mg per day for two years have not succeeded in delaying bone loss in test vertebrates. Although the additional calcium slows down loss in compact bones like the wrist, it does not seem to reach the spongy bones of the hips and spine.

Although I have stressed that you can *eat your calcium* rather than swallow it in pills, there will always be times when you will have to resort to supplements: if you dislike milk products or your system cannot tolerate them; if your menu does not include sufficient calcium-rich foods for any reason.

One thing is sure: the earlier in life you start to meet your body's need for calcium, the greater your bone mass will be and the more your body will be able to cope with normal losses caused by aging.

Of course, dairy products top the list of high-calcium foods, but they do not have a monopoly on calcium. The average amount of calcium contained in each food group is as follows:

- One serving of dairy products provides 200 mg of calcium.
- One serving of legumes provides 60 mg of calcium.
- One serving of vegetables provides 44 mg of calcium.
- One serving of meat, poultry, or fish provides 31 mg of calcium.
- One serving of fruit provides 21 mg of calcium.
- One serving of grain products provides 20 mg of calcium.

Many types of fish and vegetables exceed the group average and are your best investments.

If you are looking for exceptional calcium investments, you will have to use dairy products. However, other foods deserve special mention. Some can be eaten every day (*), while others can be added to your weekly menu.

- 5 dried figs provide 135 mg of calcium.

- 125 g (1/2 cup) cooked sweetened rhubarb provides 184 mg of calcium.
- 190 g (1 cup) cooked broccoli provides 187 mg of calcium.
* • 2 tbsp skim milk powder provides 192 mg of calcium.
- 90 g (3 oz) oil-packed sardines (with bones) provides 390 mg of calcium.
- 90 g (3 oz) canned salmon eaten with bones provides 183 mg of calcium.
* • 2 tbsp whole sesame seeds provides 176 mg of calcium.
* • 85 g (1/2 cup) cooked enriched Cream of Wheat provides 102 mg of calcium.

The "improved menu plan" presented in the concluding chapter suggests a certain number of servings for each food group that will meet not only calcium requirements but also women's three other major food priorities.

Facilitate Calcium Absorption

Calcium absorption becomes more and more difficult as a woman grows older. A pregnant woman very effectively retains the slightest amount of calcium consumed, while this is increasingly difficult for a menopausal woman. She must therefore do everything possible to integrate into her lifestyle factors that favor calcium absorption.

Factors that Facilitate Calcium Absorption (Taken as food or in the form of supplements)

- *Physical activity* is one of the best ways to promote calcium absorption. Weight-bearing exercise gives the best results: walking, skiing, skating, running, dancing, tennis, golf (no cart, please!). Research has been done to measure the impact of physical activity on bone density and suggests a minimum of three hours of adequate exercise a week.
- *Vitamin D* and calcium work together. Vitamin D is found in enriched milk, fatty fish, and fish oil. It is also conveyed by the sun's rays. A minimum of 100 IU per day is recommended. This can be found in 250 mL (8 oz) of milk. The dose of 400

IU present in many prenatal or calcium supplements is acceptable. However, you must not take too much because vitamin D in large amounts is toxic (see supplement table in the appendix).

- *Estrogen* or female hormones which cease being secreted by the ovaries at menopause have a positive effect on calcium absorption. The appropriate hormone therapy can help women absorb calcium during menopause and slow the process of bone erosion which occurs at this time of life. It is particularly recommended for women who can and want to use it in the early stages of osteoporosis.
- *Food in general* automatically stimulates the secretion of stomach acids and helps dissolve and absorb calcium supplements. Calcium supplements must always be taken at mealtime or with snacks.

Factors that Inhibit Calcium Absorption

- *Too much protein* in the diet is detrimental to calcium absorption. Too much meat or other protein causes calcium loss. A consumption of about 100 g (3 1/2 oz) of meat or fish per day, plus other vegetable protein, as well as some dairy products, will satisfy your protein requirements without harming calcium absorption.
- *Certain medications* block calcium absorption and must be avoided whenever possible:

  Aluminum-based antacids
  Furosemide (a diuretic)
  Tetracycline (an antibiotic)
  Corticosteroids
  Cholestyramine (reduces blood cholesterol levels)
  Isoniazid (anti-tuberculosis drug)

- *Large quantities of coffee* increase calcium loss. According to American researchers Heaney and Recker, each cup increases calcium requirements by 30 to 50 mg.
- *Large quantities of alcohol* block calcium absorption, affecting the liver and the metabolism of magnesium. The occasional glass of wine won't do you any harm, though.

• *Lack of physical activity* negatively affects calcium absorption. Bones that do not move lose their density.

Dietary fiber and the oxalic acid found in spinach and rhubarb have been the subject of dire warnings. Some people claim that they inhibit calcium absorption. Based on a survey of the research done on the issue, we may conclude that when there is enough calcium in the diet, the body quickly adapts to an intake of 25 to 30 g of fiber per day.

COOKING WITH CALCIUM

• Use grated cheese instead of butter on steamed vegetables, casseroles, and soups.
• Lighten your salad dressings by replacing some of the mayonnaise with yogurt, then adjust seasonings.
• Spread sandwiches with ricotta cheese instead of mayonnaise.
• Sweeten plain yogurt with blackstrap molasses instead of honey or maple syrup; 15 mL (1 tbsp) contains 137 mg of calcium.
• Use sesame butter instead of peanut butter; made with unhulled seeds, it is very high in calcium.
• Grind sesame seeds and mix with yogurt or fruit compote or sprinkle over your oatmeal. Ground seeds are easier to absorb.
• Add skim milk powder to quiche, milkshakes, rolled oats (before cooking), soups, muffin batter. Each tablespoon contains nearly 100 mg of calcium.

Nutrient Tables: Calcium

The following charts provide comprehensive information on the calcium content of the major food categories: bread and cereals, fruit, vegetables, meat, fish and poultry, legumes, milk and milk products, nuts and seeds, spices and herbs. Among all the foods listed, some are labeled "best food investments" because of their exceptional calcium content in comparison with others of the same group.

These figures set the record straight but do not impose the use of a calculator every time you do your shopping list! You can easily improve your calcium intake just by choosing more often those foods that are nearer the top of the list.

BREADS AND CEREALS	QUANTITY	CALCIUM (mg)
Cream of Wheat, enriched, cooked*	121 g (1/2 cup)	102
Bran muffin	40 g (1 medium)	57
Bran cereal (All Bran)	35 g (1/2 cup)	38
Pasta, whole-wheat, uncooked	100 g (3 1/2 oz)	38
White rice, enriched, cooked	92 g (1 cup)	35
Bagel	50 g (1)	29
Pumpernickel bread	32 g (1 slice)	27
Whole-wheat bread	28 g (1 slice)	25
Brown rice, cooked	206 g (1 cup)	22
White bread, enriched	24 g (1 slice)	20
Raisin Bran	42 g (3/4 cup)	19
Rye bread	25 g (1 slice)	19
Egg noodles, enriched, cooked	169 g (1 cup)	17
Shreddies	43 g (3/4 cup)	16
Wheat germ	30 g (1/4 cup)	16
Bran flakes	40 g (3/4 cup)	15
Macaroni, enriched, cooked	148 g (1 cup)	12
Millet, dry	51 g (1/4 cup)	12
Oat flakes, cooked	123 g (1/2 cup)	10
Shredded Wheat	25 g (1 biscuit)	10
Red River cereal, cooked	125 g (1/2 cup)	9
Cream of Wheat, not enriched, cooked	121 g (1/2 cup)	5
Pearl barley, cooked	105 g (1/2 cup)	5
Wheat bran	4.2 g (1 tbsp)	4

* Best food investment

FRUIT	QUANTITY	CALCIUM (mg)
Rhubarb, cooked, sweetened*	127 g (1/2 cup)	184
Figs, dried*	95 g (5)	135
Orange	131 g (1)	48
Blackberries	152 g (1 cup)	46
Raisins	76 g (1/2 cup)	43
Pineapple, canned	164 g (1 cup)	34
Prune juice, bottled	250 mL (1 cup)	32
Cantaloupe	267 g (1/2)	28
Dates, dried	80 g (10)	27
Strawberries, fresh or frozen	157 g (1 cup)	26
Cherries, fresh	109 g (1 cup)	24
Kiwi	76 g (1 large)	24
Grape juice, bottled	250 mL (1 cup)	24
Orange juice, frozen, diluted	250 mL (1 cup)	24
Prunes, dried	40 g (5)	22
Mango	207 g (1 medium)	18
Apple juice	250 mL (1 cup)	18
Grapefruit juice, bottled	250 mL (1 cup)	18

FRUIT	QUANTITY	CALCIUM (mg)
Apricots, fresh	105 g (3)	15
Watermelon, cubed	169 g (1 cup)	13
Grapefruit	118 g (1/2)	13
Avocado	173 g (1/2)	11
Apple	138 g (1 medium)	10
Blueberries	153 g (1 cup)	9
Banana	115 g (1 medium)	7
Nectarine	136 g (1)	6
Peach	87 g (1)	5
Plum, fresh	66 g (1)	3

* Best food investment

VEGETABLES	QUANTITY	CALCIUM (mg)
Spinach, cooked*	190 g (1 cup)	278
Broccoli, cooked*	164 g (1 cup)	187
Beet greens, cooked*	145 g (1 cup)	173
Collards, cooked*	145 g (1 cup)	148
Dandelion greens, cooked*	105 g (1 cup)	147
Swiss chard, raw*	38 g (1 cup)	146
Swiss chard, cooked	185 g (1 cup)	121
Dandelion greens, raw	60 g (1 cup)	103
Mustard greens, cooked	140 g (1 cup)	103
Kale, cooked	110 g (1 cup)	94
Broccoli, raw	151 g (1 spear)	72
Sweet potato, cooked	144 g (1 cup)	70
Tomatoes, cooked, canned	254 g (1 cup)	66
Green beans, cooked	132 g (1 cup)	61
Parsnips, cooked	165 g (1 cup)	61
Brussels sprouts, cooked	165 g (1 cup)	59
Spinach, raw	59 g (1 cup)	58
Mustard greens, raw	60 g (1 cup)	58
Turnip, cooked	165 g (1 cup)	53
Carrots, cooked	165 g (1 cup)	51
Okra, cooked	84 g (1/2 cup)	50
Cabbage, shredded, raw	74 g (1 cup)	49
Beet greens, raw	60 g (1 cup)	46
Green peas, cooked	169 g (1 cup)	44
Lettuce, leaf, raw	59 g (1 cup)	40
Red cabbage, shredded, raw	74 g (1 cup)	38
Leek, cooked	124 g (1 spear)	37
Cauliflower, cooked	190 g (1 cup)	35
Cauliflower, raw	106 g (1 cup)	31
Asparagus, cooked	120 g (8 spears)	30
Winter squash, cooked	217 g (1 cup)	30
Endive, raw	50 g (1 cup)	26
Summer squash, cooked	190 g (1 cup)	25

VEGETABLES	QUANTITY	CALCIUM (mg)
Zucchini, raw	190 g (1 cup)	25
Potato, baked, with skin	206 g (1 medium)	20
Beets, cooked	180 g (1 cup)	20
Carrot, raw	72 g (1 medium)	19
Corn, frozen, cooked	173 g (1 cup)	9
Tomato, raw	123 g (1 medium)	9
Eggplant, cooked	101 g (1 cup)	6
Mushrooms, raw	74 g (1 cup)	4
Green pepper, raw	73 g (1 medium)	4
Mushrooms, cooked	41 g (1/2 cup)	3

* Best food investment

MEAT, FISH, POULTRY	QUANTITY	CALCIUM (mg)
Sardines, canned, with bones*	90 g (3 oz)	393
Salmon, canned, with bones*	90 g (3 oz)	183
Herring, canned, with bones*	90 g (3 oz)	132
Scallops, cooked	91 g (7)	104
Shrimp, canned	90 g (3 oz)	104
Oysters, raw	90 g (6 medium)	85
Lobster, canned	90 g (3 oz)	59
Clams, canned	90 g (3 oz)	50
Trout, broiled	90 g (3 oz)	47
Crab, canned	90 g (3 oz)	41
Egg, cooked	50 g (1)	28
Cod, broiled	90 g (3 oz)	28
Boston bluefish, broiled	90 g (3 oz)	26
Haddock, raw	90 g (3 oz)	20
Tuna, canned	90 g (3 oz)	18
Pork liver, cooked	90 g (3 oz)	14
Halibut, broiled	90 g (3 oz)	14
Sole, cooked	90 g (3 oz)	14
Calves' liver, cooked	90 g (3 oz)	12
Chicken liver, cooked	90 g (3 oz)	10
Veal roast, cooked	90 g (3 oz)	10
Lamb chop, lean, cooked	90 g (3 oz)	10
Pork roast, cooked	90 g (3 oz)	9
Beef, lean, cooked	90 g (3 oz)	8
Chicken, without skin, cooked	90 g (3 oz)	8
Ham, lean, cooked	90 g (3 oz)	7
Beef liver, cooked	90 g (3 oz)	6

* Best food investment

LEGUMES	QUANTITY	CALCIUM (mg)
Tofu*	120 g (4 oz)	154
Soybeans, cooked*	190 g (1 cup)	139
Pinto beans, cooked*	95 g (1 cup)	130

LEGUMES	QUANTITY	CALCIUM (mg)
White kidney beans, cooked	137 g (1 cup)	98
Chickpeas, cooked	211 g (1 cup)	84
Red kidney beans, cooked	195 g (1 cup)	78
Lima beans, cooked	180 g (1 cup)	58
Lentils, cooked	211 g (1 cup)	53
Lima beans, frozen, cooked	201 g (1 cup)	50
Black beans, cooked	200 g (1 cup)	45
Black-eyed peas, cooked	264 g (1 cup)	43
Split peas, cooked	211 g (1 cup)	23

* Best food investment

MILK AND MILK PRODUCTS	QUANTITY	CALCIUM (mg)
Skim milk powder*	8 g (2 tbsp)	192
Ricotta	130 g (1/2 cup)	337
Skim milk	250 mL (1 cup)	317
2% milk	250 mL (1 cup)	315
Whole milk	250 mL (1 cup)	306
Buttermilk	250 mL (1 cup)	299
Gruyère	30 g (1 oz)	287
Yogurt, plain	129 g (1/2 cup)	237
Cheddar	30 g (1 oz)	216
Provolone	30 g (1 oz)	214
Gouda	30 g (1 oz)	214
Edam	30 g (1 oz)	207
Colby	30 g (1 oz)	206
Brick	30 g (1 oz)	191
Roquefort	30 g (1 oz)	188
Mozzarella, partially skimmed	30 g (1 oz)	183
Sliced cheese (processed)	30 g (1 oz)	174
Blue	30 g (1 oz)	156
Mozzarella	30 g (1 oz)	147
Swiss cheese	30 g (1 oz)	144
Feta	30 g (1 oz)	140
Camembert	30 g (1 oz)	110
Ice cream, vanilla	70 g (1/2 cup)	92
Cottage cheese (2%)	120 g (1/2 cup)	77
Brie	30 g (1 oz)	52

* Best food investment

NUTS AND SEEDS	QUANTITY	CALCIUM (mg)
Sesame seeds, whole, dried*	9.5 g (1 tbsp)	88
Sesame butter, stone ground*	14 g (1 tbsp)	63
Almonds	15	35
Brazil nuts	4 large	31

NUTS AND SEEDS	QUANTITY	CALCIUM (mg)
Hazelnuts (filberts)	10	29
Pistachios	30	24
Sunflower seeds, dried	18 g (2 tbsp)	20
Cashews	14 large	13
Walnuts	5 halves	12
Pecans	16	10
Peanut butter	16 g (1 tbsp)	5
Coconut, sweetened, dried	25 g (1/4 cup)	3

* Best food investment

SPICES AND HERBS	QUANTITY	CALCIUM (mg)
Poppy seed	5 mL (1 tsp)	41
Celery seed	5 mL (1 tsp)	35
Dill seed	5 mL (1 tsp)	32
Savory	5 mL (1 tsp)	30
Basil	5 mL (1 tsp)	30
Cinnamon	5 mL (1 tsp)	28
Thyme	5 mL (1 tsp)	26
Oregano	5 mL (1 tsp)	24
Fennel seed	5 mL (1 tsp)	24
Cumin seed	5 mL (1 tsp)	20
Cloves, ground	5 mL (1 tsp)	14
Allspice	5 mL (1 tsp)	13

10

More Magnesium!

INCREASE INTAKE OF
MAGNESIUM-RICH FOODS AND
FACILITATE MAGNESIUM ABSORPTION

Cardiovascular disease is the primary cause of death in women over the age of fifty. Since the protective role played by magnesium in such cases is generally overlooked, it is appropriate that we discuss it here. When women increase their calcium intake, they may not be aware that they are automatically increasing their need for magnesium. It is therefore essential that magnesium play a more important role in their diet!

Magnesium Destroyed by Processing

Today, food contains less magnesium than it did a century ago. With the advent of refined, sweetened, and fat-laden foods, magnesium has gradually disappeared from our food supply. Food processing has had a disastrous effect on magnesium. White rice has only one-third of the magnesium contained in brown rice. A slice of white bread has only one-quarter of the magnesium in whole-wheat bread. All products made with white flour suffer the same fate!

While serious magnesium deficiency will result in heart-rate problems and convulsions, more widespread and less severe deficiencies attract little attention since they are not easy to detect. A diet composed mainly of refined foods and high in calcium only increases the risk of magnesium deficiency in many women.

Sixty per cent of the body's magnesium is found in the bones and nearly forty per cent in the muscle cells. Unlike calcium, which is quickly released by the bones in an emergency situation, magnesium is relatively stable. However, it is hyperactive at the cell level, permitting protein, carbohydrates, and fats to be transformed into energy.

Needs Change Over the Life Cycle

First, refer to the table at the end of this section.

Proportionally, *teenage girls* need more magnesium than adult women, but their current average magnesium intake leaves a great deal to be desired! A shortage of magnesium and vitamin B_6 has been related, among other things, to premenstrual tension, a common problem at this age.

Pregnant women need a great deal of magnesium to be able to meet the growing demands of the fetus over nine months.

Nursing mothers supply their babies with about 40 mg of magnesium per day in their milk. To avoid dipping into their own reserves, these women must increase their magnesium intake.

Vegetarian women are the best off! They have the same requirements as their meat-eating sisters, but consume far more magnesium because their diet is so rich in vegetables and whole grains. This extra magnesium seems to result in lower cholesterol levels and a lower incidence of hypertension.

Adult and menopausal women trying to consume 1,000 mg of calcium per day must also readjust their intake of magnesium to maintain a calcium/magnesium ratio of two to one. To do so, they should aim for 400 to 500 mg of magnesium per day. Canada's recommended intakes do not yet reflect these suggestions, but this is the level of magnesium recommended in the United States and Europe and by researchers who have studied the issue.

Hospitalized women seem to be the most vulnerable to magnesium deficiency. In fact, one hospital patient in ten suffers from such a shortage. A woman recovering from surgery or taking diuretics must watch her magnesium intake and use a supplement if necessary.

Female athletes have particularly high magnesium requirements. Marathoners who run in the heat lose more magnesium than under normal circumstances. Exceptional physical effort also causes magnesium loss. Beware!

Magnesium

AGE	ACTUAL INTAKE*	RECOMMENDED INTAKE**	
		CANADA (1983)	U.S.A. (1980)
13-15		200 mg	300 mg
16-18	190-210 mg	215 mg	300 mg
19-24		200 mg	300 mg
25-49	210-220 mg	200 mg	300 mg
50-74	185 mg	210 mg	300 mg
75+	—	220 mg	300 mg
Pregnancy 1st Trimester	—	215 mg	450 mg
2nd Trimester	—	220 mg	450 mg
3rd Trimester	—	225 mg	450 mg
Lactation	—	280 mg	450 mg

* Figures taken from research cited in references in Chapter 1.

** The recommended allowances or nutrient intakes vary from country to country. These figures reflect the philosophy of one group of experts and may not correspond with those of another group.
  They are revised and updated periodically, based on the most current scientific research.

Where to Find Magnesium

Magnesium is found in a number of different foods. Try to take in *between 400 and 500 mg of magnesium per day*.

These figures are much closer to the U.S. recommendations than they are to the Canadian. To attain these levels, there is no need to eat a huge quantity of food, but rather increase your intake of whole grains, always include a variety of fruits and add vegetables, and legumes, which are super-rich in magnesium. The average amounts of magnesium contained in each food group are as follows:

• One serving of grain products provides 35 mg of magnesium.
• One serving of meat, poultry, or fish provides 25 mg of magnesium.

- One serving of legumes provides 90 mg of magnesium.
- One serving of dairy products provides 12 mg of magnesium.
- One serving of fruit provides 22 mg of magnesium.
- One serving of vegetables provides 31 mg of magnesium.

Many foods exceed the average for the respective food group and are your best food investments. Some exceptional food investments can be part of your daily menu (*), while others can be added to your weekly or monthly menu.

* • 35 g (1/2 cup) bran cereal contains 123 mg of magnesium.
  - 30 g (1/4 cup) wheat germ contains 125 mg of magnesium.
  - 190 g (1 cup) cooked spinach contains 130 mg of magnesium.
  - 185 g (1 cup) cooked Swiss chard contains 150 mg of magnesium.
* • 18 g (2 tbsp) sunflower seeds contains 66 mg of magnesium.
* • 10 g (2 tbsp) unhulled sesame seeds contains 64 mg of magnesium.

Facilitate Magnesium Absorption

Proper magnesium absorption and a healthy diet go together.

Factors that Facilitate Magnesium Absorption (in food or in supplement form)

- An acid environment facilitates magnesium absorption. In other words, taking magnesium with a meal helps its absorption since it stimulates the secretion of stomach acid.
- The presence of vitamin D and lactose in the diet is also favorable to the absorption of magnesium.

Factors that Inhibit Magnesium Absorption

- Too much calcium simultaneously increases both magnesium loss and magnesium requirements. Calcium and magnesium compete for the same carriers in the intestine. They inhibit each other's absorption. An increase in calcium intake neces-

sarily requires an adjustment of magnesium intake; the ideal ratio is two to one: two parts calcium to one part magnesium.
- *Excess fat* is bad since it reduces the body's ability to absorb magnesium in the intestine.
- *Excess sugar and alcohol* increase both magnesium loss and magnesium requirements.
- *Excess protein* decreases the absorption of both magnesium and calcium.
- *Diuretics* cause magnesium loss.

Dietary fiber does not impair magnesium absorption. Based on a survey of the research done on the issue, we may conclude that when there is enough magnesium in the diet, the body quickly adapts to an intake of 25 to 30 g of fiber per day.

COOKING WITH MAGNESIUM

- Use wheat germ instead of bread crumbs in meat loaf or to coat fish fillets or chicken breasts.
- Keep some finely chopped figs on hand; add them to plain yogurt, rolled oats, or dry cereal.
- Add a few Swiss chard or dandelion leaves to a green salad.
- Instead of iceberg lettuce in your sandwich, use some fresh spinach leaves.
- Add some toasted or chopped almonds or sunflower seeds to a tossed green salad.
- Serve broccoli two or three times a week: steamed, sautéed in a wok, in salad or in soup.
- Add lentils or soybeans to spaghetti sauce or shepherd's pie.
- Make a well-seasoned lentil soup. Serve with lots of fresh minced parsley.
- Make tofu a staple food in your diet.
- Sprinkle your morning cereal with sesame or sunflower seeds.
- Add a handful of almonds or sunflower seeds to your snack of fresh fruit.
- Add a few spoonfuls of wheat germ or sesame seeds to freshly cooked brown rice.

Nutrient Tables: Magnesium

The following charts provide comprehensive information on the magnesium content of the major food categories: bread and cereals, fruit, vegetables, meat, fish and poultry, legumes, milk and milk products, nuts and seeds, spices and herbs. Among all the foods listed, some are labeled "best food investments" because of their exceptional magnesium content in comparison with others of the same group.

These figures set the record straight but do not impose the use of a calculator every time you make up your shopping list! You can easily improve your magnesium intake just by choosing more often those foods that are nearer the top of the list.

BREADS AND CEREALS	QUANTITY	MAGNESIUM (mg)
Wheat germ*	30 g (1/4 cup)	125
Bran cereal (All Bran)*	35 g (1/2 cup)	123
Millet, dry	51 g (1/4 cup)	94
Bran flakes	40 g (3/4 cup)	77
Pasta, whole wheat, uncooked	100 g (3 1/2 oz)	69
Oat flakes, cooked	123 g (1/2 cup)	59
Brown rice, cooked	206 g (1 cup)	57
Shredded Wheat	25 g (1 biscuit)	43
Shreddies	43 g (3/4 cup)	40
Bran muffin	40 g (1 medium)	38
Raisin Bran	42 g (3/4 cup)	32
Macaroni, enriched, cooked	148 g (1 cup)	28
Pumpernickel bread	32 g (1 slice)	23
Whole-wheat bread	28 g (1 slice)	22
Pearl barley, cooked	105 g (1/2 cup)	18
Wheat bran	4.2 g (1 tbsp)	16
White rice, enriched, cooked	92 g (1 cup)	16
Rye bread	25 g (1 slice)	10
White bread, enriched	24 g (1 slice)	6
Cream of Wheat, enriched, cooked	121 g (1/2 cup)	6
Cream of Wheat, not enriched, cooked	121 g (1/2 cup)	5
Egg noodles, enriched, cooked	169 g (1 cup)	–
Red River cereal, cooked	125 g (1/2 cup)	–
Bagel	50 g (1)	–

(–) Value not available in references consulted.
* *Best food investment*

FRUIT	QUANTITY	MAGNESIUM (mg)
Figs, dried	95 g (5)	55
Raisins	76 g (1/2 cup)	51
Blackberries	152 g (1 cup)	43
Avocado	173 g (1/2)	40
Banana	115 g (1 medium)	39
Prune juice, bottled	250 mL (1 cup)	36
Dates, dried	80 g (10)	29
Cantaloupe	267 g (1/2)	29
Orange juice, frozen, diluted	250 mL (1 cup)	27
Grapefruit juice, bottled	250 mL (1 cup)	26
Grape juice, bottled	250 mL (1 cup)	24

FRUIT	QUANTITY	MAGNESIUM (mg)
Kiwi	76 g (1 large)	23
Prunes, dried	40 g (5)	20
Pineapple, canned	164 g (1 cup)	20
Watermelon, cubed	169 g (1 cup)	19
Strawberries, fresh or frozen	157 g (1 cup)	18
Mango	207 g (1 medium)	18
Rhubarb, cooked, sweetened	127 g (1/2 cup)	15
Orange	131 g (1)	14
Apricots, fresh	105 g (3)	13
Nectarine	136 g (1)	11
Cherries, fresh	109 g (1 cup)	10
Apple juice	250 mL (1 cup)	10
Grapefruit	118 g (1/2)	10
Blueberries	153 g (1 cup)	8
Apple	138 g (1 medium)	7
Plum, fresh	66 g (1)	6
Peach	87 g (1)	6

VEGETABLES	QUANTITY	MAGNESIUM (mg)
Swiss chard, cooked*	185 g (1 cup)	150
Spinach, frozen, cooked*	190 g (1 cup)	130
Collards, cooked	145 g (1 cup)	121
Broccoli, cooked	164 g (1 cup)	98
Beet greens, cooked	145 g (1 cup)	97
Beets, cooked	180 g (1 cup)	67
Green peas, cooked	169 g (1 cup)	66
Potato, baked, with skin	206 g (1 medium)	55
Corn, frozen, cooked	173 g (1 cup)	55
Parsnips, cooked	165 g (1 cup)	48
Okra, cooked	84 g (1/2 cup)	46
Spinach, raw	59 g (1 cup)	44
Sweet potato, cooked	144 g (1 cup)	42
Broccoli, raw	151 g (1 spear)	38
Green beans, cooked	132 g (1 cup)	35
Brussels sprouts, cooked	165 g (1 cup)	33
Zucchini, raw	190 g (1 cup)	32
Swiss chard, raw	38 g (1 cup)	30
Tomatoes, cooked, canned	254 g (1 cup)	30
Beet greens, raw	60 g (1 cup)	28
Turnip, cooked	165 g (1 cup)	26
Kale, cooked	110 g (1 cup)	23
Carrot, raw	72 g (1 medium)	23
Asparagus, cooked	120 g (8 spears)	22
Dandelion greens, raw	60 g (1 cup)	21
Mustard greens, cooked	140 g (1 cup)	21
Summer squash, cooked	190 g (1 cup)	21

VEGETABLES	QUANTITY	MAGNESIUM (mg)
Tomato, raw	123 g (1 medium)	21
Mustard greens, raw	60 g (1 cup)	18
Leek, cooked	124 g (1 spear)	17
Winter squash, cooked	217 g (1 cup)	17
Eggplant, cooked	101 g (1 cup)	16
Cauliflower, raw	106 g (1 cup)	15
Cauliflower, cooked	190 g (1 cup)	14
Carrots, cooked	165 g (1 cup)	14
Green pepper, raw	73 g (1 medium)	13
Cabbage, shredded, raw	74 g (1 cup)	13
Red cabbage, shredded, raw	74 g (1 cup)	11
Mushrooms, raw	74 g (1 cup)	7
Lettuce, leaf, raw	59 g (1 cup)	7
Mushrooms, cooked	41 g (1/2 cup)	5
Endive, raw	50 g (1 cup)	4
Dandelion greens, cooked	105 g (1 cup)	–

* *Best food investment*
(–) Value not available in references consulted

MEAT, FISH, POULTRY	QUANTITY	MAGNESIUM (mg)
Sardines, canned, with bones	90 g (3 oz)	47
Shrimp, canned	90 g (3 oz)	44
Scallops, cooked	91 g (7)	33
Crab, canned	90 g (3 oz)	31
Lobster, canned	90 g (3 oz)	31
Oysters, raw	90 g (6 medium)	29
Herring, canned	90 g (3 oz)	27
Salmon, canned, with bones	90 g (3 oz)	26
Veal roast, cooked	90 g (3 oz)	25
Tuna, canned	90 g (3 oz)	25
Haddock, raw	90 g (3 oz)	24
Cod, broiled	90 g (3 oz)	24
Chicken, without skin, cooked	90 g (3 oz)	23
Pork roast, cooked	90 g (3 oz)	22
Lamb chop, lean, cooked	90 g (3 oz)	22
Calves' liver, cooked	90 g (3 oz)	22
Halibut, broiled	90 g (3 oz)	21
Ham, lean, cooked	90 g (3 oz)	20
Chicken liver, cooked	90 g (3 oz)	19
Beef, cooked	90 g (3 oz)	18
Beef liver, cooked	90 g (3 oz)	17
Pork liver, cooked	90 g (3 oz)	13
Egg, cooked	50 g (1)	12
Clams, canned	90 g (3 oz)	–
Trout, broiled	90 g (3 oz)	–
Boston bluefish, broiled	90 g (3 oz)	–
Sole, cooked	90 g (3 oz)	–

(–) Value not available in references consulted.

LEGUMES	QUANTITY	MAGNESIUM (mg)
Tofu	120 g (4 oz)	133
Lima beans, cooked	180 g (1 cup)	126
Split peas, cooked	211 g (1 cup)	108
Lima beans, frozen, cooked	201 g (1 cup)	100
White kidney beans, cooked	137 g (1 cup)	90
Black-eyed peas, cooked	264 g (1 cup)	90
Red kidney beans, cooked	195 g (1 cup)	88
Black beans, cooked	200 g (1 cup)	42
Lentils, cooked	211 g (1 cup)	36
Soybeans, cooked	190 g (1 cup)	–
Pinto beans, cooked	95 g (1 cup)	–
Chickpeas, cooked	211 g (1 cup)	–

(–) Value not available in references consulted.

MILK AND MILK PRODUCTS	QUANTITY	MAGNESIUM (mg)
Skim milk	250 mL (1 cup)	28
Whole milk	250 mL (1 cup)	28
Buttermilk	250 mL (1 cup)	27
2% milk	250 mL (1 cup)	26
Yogurt, plain	129 g (1/2 cup)	23
Ricotta	130 g (1/2 cup)	18
Skim milk powder	8 g (2 tbsp)	17
Cheddar	30 g (1 oz)	13
Gruyère	30 g (1 oz)	11
Ice cream, vanilla	70 g (1/2 cup)	10
Gouda	30 g (1 oz)	9
Edam	30 g (1 oz)	8
Provolone	30 g (1 oz)	8
Roquefort	30 g (1 oz)	8
Colby	30 g (1 oz)	8
Cottage cheese (2%)	120 g (1/2 cup)	7
Mozzarella, partially skimmed	30 g (1 oz)	7
Brick	30 g (1 oz)	7
Blue	30 g (1 oz)	7
Camembert	30 g (1 oz)	6
Sliced cheese (processed)	30 g (1 oz)	6
Mozzarella	30 g (1 oz)	6
Brie	30 g (1 oz)	6
Feta	30 g (1 oz)	5
Swiss cheese	30 g (1 oz)	5

NUTS AND SEEDS	QUANTITY	MAGNESIUM (mg)
Cashews*	14 large	75
Sunflower seeds, dried*	18 g (2 tbsp)	66
Sesame seeds, whole, dried*	9.5 g (1 tbsp)	64

NUTS AND SEEDS	QUANTITY	MAGNESIUM (mg)
Almonds	15	41
Pecans	16	36
Brazil nuts	4 large	34
Hazelnuts (filberts)	10	28
Peanut butter	16 g (1 tbsp)	28
Pistachios	30	24
Walnuts	5 halves	17
Coconut, sweetened, dried	25 g (1/4 cup)	14
Sesame butter, stone ground	14 g (1 tbsp)	14

* Best food investment

SPICES AND HERBS	QUANTITY	MAGNESIUM (mg)
Poppy seed	5 mL (1 tsp)	9
Celery seed	5 mL (1 tsp)	9
Cumin seed	5 mL (1 tsp)	8
Fennel seed	5 mL (1 tsp)	8
Cloves, ground	5 mL (1 tsp)	6
Basil	5 mL (1 tsp)	6
Savory	5 mL (1 tsp)	5
Dill seed	5 mL (1 tsp)	5
Oregano	5 mL (1 tsp)	4
Allspice	5 mL (1 tsp)	3
Thyme	5 mL (1 tsp)	3
Cinnamon	5 mL (1 tsp)	1

ON
YOUR
WAY!

11

Menus that Meet the Challenge

There are two ways to come to terms with women's four main dietary priorities: eat a 2,500 calorie-per-day low nutrient diet *or* concentrate on foods that are the best health investments.

Since I know very few women who would be interested in the first suggestion, I recommend the second option, and encourage you to gradually adopt the "improved menu plan" you will find on the next few pages. These menus provide no more than 1,500 to 1,700 calories per day (which most women already eat) and feature foods that are highest in vitamins and minerals.

The suggested meals are not hard to plan or cook. Moderation, a watchword that is unfortunately not well understood by proponents of extremist diets, is the key. The menu plan is based on foods that are not highly refined, and are spread over the day to meet all of women's nutritional needs.

The improved menu plan includes:

- At least *three servings of fruit* per day. Choose the freshest fruit at the market. The ripest fruit is also the sweetest. Eat at least two that are high in vitamin C (pages 112 and 113) to facilitate iron absorption. Give priority to fruit rather than fruit juice.

- At least *three servings of vegetables* per day. Choose the freshest vegetables at the market; pick brightly colored and dark green vegetables. Avoid any that are pale and limp. Eat at least one serving of raw vegetables; never overcook the others! Include a vegetable that is high in vitamin C (pages 112 and 113) in your third meal to improve iron absorption.

- *Three servings of dairy products* per day. Give priority to low-fat products like skim milk and partly skimmed milk, yogurt and low-fat cheeses. Drink at least one glass of milk per day for its vitamin D content.

- *One serving of legumes or tofu* per day. They contain exceptionally high levels of iron and magnesium. To save time, use canned legumes (chickpeas, kidney beans, pinto beans). Add them to your daily diet gradually.

- *One serving of meat, poultry, or fish* per day (eat fish or seafood two or three times a week). Give priority to fresh lean meat, regularly eat liver and grain-fed poultry when available. Vary the fish and seafood you eat—don't forget fatty fishes like salmon, trout, and mackerel. Eat about four whole eggs a week, cooked without fat: poached or boiled.

- At least *four servings of whole grain products* per day (see the list below) including whole grain bread, brown rice, whole grain cereals, whole-wheat pasta. These foods contribute more minerals and less fat and calories than cookies, crackers, and the like.

- *A maximum of 30 ml (2 tbsp) visible fat* per day, including 15 ml polyunsaturated fat (see pages 103-105).

Whole Grains and Whole Grain Products

WHOLE GRAINS	LIQUID REQUIRED FOR COOKING	COOKING TIME
175 g (1 cup) wheat	750 mL (3 cups)	2 hours
170 g (1 cup) bulghur	500 mL (2 cups)	15-25 minutes
170 g (1 cup) couscous	250 mL (1 cup)	Soak 10 minutes in boiling liquid
160 g (1 cup) buckwheat (kasha)	500 mL (2 cups)	15 minutes
200 g (1 cup) millet	750 mL (3 cups)	25 minutes
200 g (1 cup) pot barley	1,000 mL (4 cups)	60 minutes
120 g (1 cup) corn meal	1,000 mL (4 cups)	25-30 minutes
185 g (1 cup) brown rice	500 mL (2 cups)	45 minutes
160 g (1 cup) wild rice (soak for 8 hours)	1,000 mL (4 cups)	20 minutes

Whole Grain Cereals Requiring Cooking	*Ready to Eat*	*Whole Grain Products*
Rolled oats	Shredded Wheat	Whole-wheat bread
	Shreddies	Whole-wheat pasta

Whole Grain Cereals Requiring Cooking	Ready to Eat	Whole Grain Products
Rye flakes	All Bran	Dark rye bread
Red River cereal	Grapenuts	(pumpernickel)
	Bran Buds	Bran muffin
	Natural bran	Oatmeal muffin
	Weetabix	Whole-wheat pita bread
	Muesli	Multigrain bread
	Pep	

It is important to give top billing to foods that exceed their food group average in nutrient content. Remember that the alternative approach calls for eating better, but does not recommend any drastic or rapid changes.

Teenagers can increase suggested serving sizes if necessary, but this basic menu plan should meet all their needs.

Lacto-ovo-vegetarian women who do not eat meat or fish should add an additional serving of grain products to meet all their dietary needs.

Strict vegetarian women who do not eat dairy products should take a vitamin D and calcium supplement. A vitamin B_{12} supplement is also required when pregnant or nursing. They should also add a handful of nuts or seeds each day in order to get enough calories.

Pregnant women who have greater dietary needs should add at least one serving of dairy products and one serving of grains to the basic menu plan. Serving size can be increased according to appetite. Toward the end of the pregnancy, when the baby is bigger, healthy snacks between meals are helpful to avoid eating large, heavy meals.

Nursing mothers should continue to eat as much as when they were pregnant. Healthy snacks between meals will keep energy levels high.

Older women who eat less have every interest in regularly choosing "exceptional food investments" to compensate for reduced quantities.

If you would like to make certain changes in the menu plan—for example, to omit the legumes or decrease the amount of grains, it can be done so long as you make use of exceptional iron and magnesium investments to compensate. If you do not eat a third serving of dairy products, replace it with some other exceptional calcium investments.

IMPROVED MENU PLAN

This menu plan opens the door to more nutritious meals from dawn to dusk! Based on a holistic approach to food, it takes into consideration women's dietary needs and pays special attention to foods that are the best nutritional investments.

The menu plan is based on the daily minimum of:

- three servings of fruit
- three servings of vegetables
- three servings of dairy products
- four servings of whole grain products
- one serving of legumes or tofu
- one serving of meat or fish.

The vegetarian menu plan contains an additional serving of grain products.

The menu plan includes a few tips which may increase your intake and absorption of calcium, iron, and magnesium. Suggested dishes can be added gradually to your regular menu. Or use them as inspiration and create your own new recipes.

Bon appétit!

DAY 1

Breakfast
Orange sections
Bran cereal sprinkled with chopped almonds
Partly skimmed milk

Lunch
Thick lentil soup
Dark green salad
Instant homemade vinaigrette (p. 53)
Whole-wheat bread
Strawberries and yogurt

Dinner
Meat loaf
Brown rice pilaf with mushrooms and wheat germ
Crunchy broccoli salad (lightly cooked)
Whole-wheat bread
Bananas *en papillotte**

Snack
Milk and sunflower seeds

DAY 2

Breakfast
Bowl of yogurt
Strawberries in season and sunflower seeds
Bran muffin or whole-wheat toast

Lunch
Raw vegetables
Minestrone soup with kidney beans (p. 82)
Cheese and whole-wheat bread
Kiwi

Dinner
Chinese-style liver (p. 111)
Brown rice with pesto (p. 51)
Cole slaw
Whole-wheat bread
Fresh pineapple wedges

Snack
Glass of milk

---

*For each serving, slice a banana in two lengthwise. Place on a sheet of aluminum foil big enough to wrap in. Sprinkle banana with 1 or 2 tbsp of orange juice. Wrap in foil, dull side out, place in baking dish, and bake at 400°F for 15 minutes. Serve with yogurt if desired.

DAY 3

Breakfast
Half grapefruit
Oatmeal with added skim milk powder, figs, and cinnamon
Partly skimmed milk

Lunch
Pita bread with chickpea salad
Green pepper strips
Pear and vanilla yogurt

Dinner
Herb-steamed salmon steak (p. 57)
Carrots and snow peas
Millet with parsley
Whole-wheat bread
Half cantaloupe with strawberry coulis (p. 56)

Snack
Cheese and grapes

DAY 4

Breakfast
Orange juice
Whole-wheat bread with cheese

Lunch
Raw cauliflower with yogurt dip (p. 55 or p. 56)
Salmon sandwich with spinach leaves
Slice of watermelon

Dinner
Whole-wheat pasta
Lentil sauce
Dark green salad (lamb's lettuce, watercress, and romaine lettuce)
Rhubarb and strawberry compote

Snack
Yogurt and toasted almonds

DAY 5

Breakfast
Cottage cheese
Orange sections, dried fruit, wheat germ
Whole-wheat toast

Lunch
Sliced chicken and julienned vegetables in
whole-wheat pita bread
Banana milkshake

Dinner
Spinach and tofu quiche (p. 152)
Green beans vinaigrette
Whole-wheat bread
Clementines

Snack
Glass of milk

VEGETARIAN DAY (6)

Breakfast
Orange-prune juice
Enriched Cream of Wheat with chopped hazelnuts
Partly skimmed milk
Whole-wheat toast

Lunch
Raw vegetables
Broccoli soup (p. 150)
Cheese and dark rye bread
Nuts and dried fruit

Dinner
Shepherd's pie with lentils (p. 151)
Tomatoes vinaigrette
Whole-wheat bread
Cantaloupe and green grapes

Snack
Glass of milk

DAY 7

Breakfast
Half grapefruit
Poached egg on whole-wheat toast
Glass of milk

Lunch
Chickpea soup or chickpeas vinaigrette
Lean roast beef sandwich on whole-wheat bread with mustard
and lettuce
Orange or tangerine

Dinner
Green salad with vinaigrette
Baked or poached white fish with broiled tomato
Apple and slice of cheese

Snack
Glass of milk

SOME MENU RECIPES

BROCCOLI SOUP

Preparation time: 5 minutes
Cooking time: 15 to 20 minutes
Makes 4 servings

300 g (2 cups) broccoli florets, chopped
250 mL (1 cup) chicken or vegetable stock
250 mL (1 cup) partly skimmed milk

10 mL (2 tsp) sunflower oil
Thyme to taste
Salt and pepper

In a large pot, cook broccoli in chicken or vegetable stock for 15 to 20 minutes. Pour half the mixture into a blender or food processor and purée until smooth. Repeat with the other half. Pour back into the pot and heat, gradually adding the milk and oil. Season to taste. Serve hot.

SHEPHERD'S PIE WITH LENTILS

Cooking time for lentils: 45 minutes
Preparation time for other ingredients: 15 minutes
Cooking time: about 40 minutes
Makes 4 servings

225 g (1 cup) dried green lentils
1 large onion, peeled and finely chopped
1 clove garlic, minced
125 g (1 1/2 cups) fresh mushrooms, sliced
170 g (1 cup) corn kernels
15 mL (1 tbsp) corn or sunflower oil
30 mL (2 tbsp) tomato paste
Pinch of thyme
Salt and pepper to taste
4 cooked potatoes, mashed

Lentils do not require soaking before cooking. Cover the lentils with cold water and simmer for about 45 minutes, or until soft. Drain well.

While lentils are simmering, cook onion, garlic, and mushrooms until soft. Add corn, cooked lentils, tomato paste, and seasonings to taste. Mix well and pour into an ovenproof dish. Cover with mashed potatoes and bake at 400°F for 30 to 40 minutes.

SPINACH AND TOFU QUICHE

Preparation time: 20 minutes
Cooking time: about 40 minutes
Makes 6 servings

2 onions, peeled and thinly sliced
5 mL (1 tsp) corn oil
4 g (1 tsp) butter
300 g (10 oz) fresh spinach
Pinch of nutmeg
2 large eggs
360 g (12 oz) tofu
45 g (1/2 cup) grated Parmesan cheese
Salt and pepper to taste
1 ripe tomato, sliced
1 23 cm (9") precooked whole-wheat pie shell

Cook onions in oil and butter over low heat until soft. Drain and pour into pie shell. Wash and cook spinach for about 5 minutes, or until wilted. Drain; chop and place in a large bowl. Sprinkle with nutmeg to taste. Beat eggs, tofu, and cheese together until smooth. Add to the spinach. Season with salt and pepper and pour over the onions. Garnish with tomato slices and bake for about 40 minutes at 375°F or until set. Let stand 5 to 10 minutes before serving.

Excellent with fresh tomato sauce.
(If you prefer to skip the crust, you can make a flan with the same ingredients. Cooking time will be the same.)

A LAST WORD

There was much that I needed to say!

My first objective was to underline the differences between men's and women's eating patterns, nutritional requirements, health problems, and social restrictions.

By painting a rather bleak picture of women's current nutritional status, I wanted them to understand that it is likely to worsen if they do not do something about it!

If I then put weight-loss diets on trial, and found them wanting, it was in part to comfort all those women who have despaired of losing weight, and to help explain why their efforts have not met with success. *My dream is to see women go on a diet strike once and for all!* Then, and only then, will they be able to rebuild a happy relationship with themselves and with food.

I have also criticized the most popular unconventional diets, some of which are causing severe dietary imbalances in women unaware of the risks associated with such extreme approaches.

Finally, I wanted to deal with the real problems affecting women and their eating habits: lack of time, eating out, living alone. . . . I have tried to give ample suggestions that can easily be adapted to daily living.

I don't believe in absolute answers, miracle solutions, or abrupt changes in food habits. I have tried to provide a flexible, painless transition to better eating habits by suggesting simple, long-term solutions that meet women's needs.

I sincerely hope that this book will light the spark that will begin the process of changes toward better eating for each and every one of my readers.

Appendix

The Other Missing Nutrients (Tables 1 and 2)
Supplements (Tables 3 and 4)

Among other nutrients that are inadequate in many women's menus, researchers have noted zinc and vitamin B_6 in particular.

As mentioned in the introduction to Chapter 7 (page 98), I do not include these two nutrients as separate priorities because my calculations show that the best food investment route for iron, calcium and magnesium leads automatically to an adequate intake of zinc and vitamin B_6.

Having demonstrated the simplified way of eating a healthier diet, I'm sure that many women will be interested in knowing which foods are rich in these two nutrients, such information being difficult to find—even for a dietitian! This explains the presence of the following charts.

Table 1

BREADS AND CEREALS	QUANTITY	ZINC (mg)
Wheat germ*	30 g (1/4 cup)	4.7
Bran cereal (All Bran)*	35 g (1/2 cup)	2.7
Pasta, whole-wheat, uncooked	100 g (3 1/2 oz)	2
Bran flakes	40 g (3/4 cup)	1.9
Brown rice, cooked	206 g (1 cup)	1.2
Bran muffin	40 g (1 medium)	1.1
Millet, dry	51 g (1/4 cup)	0.9
Shreddies	43 g (3/4 cup)	0.9
Macaroni, enriched, cooked	148 g (1 cup)	0.7
Shredded Wheat	25 g (1 biscuit)	0.6
Oat flakes, cooked	123 g (1/2 cup)	0.6
White rice, enriched, cooked	92 g (1 cup)	0.6
Pearl barley, cooked	105 g (1/2 cup)	0.6
Raisin Bran	42 g (3/4 cup)	0.6
Bagel	50 g (1)	0.5
Whole-wheat bread	28 g (1 slice)	0.5
Rye bread	25 g (1 slice)	0.4
Wheat bran	4.2 g (1 tbsp)	0.3
White bread, enriched	24 g (1 slice)	0.2
Cream of Wheat, enriched, cooked	121 g (1/2 cup)	0.2
Cream of Wheat, not enriched, cooked	121 g (1/2 cup)	0.2
Pumpernickel bread	32 g (1 slice)	0.1
Egg noodles, enriched, cooked	169 g (1 cup)	–
Red River cereal, cooked	125 g (1/2 cup)	–

(–) Value not available in references consulted.
* *Best food investment*

FRUIT	QUANTITY	ZINC (mg)
Prune juice, bottled	250 mL (1 cup)	0.6
Figs, dried	95 g (5)	0.5
Avocado	173 g (1/2)	0.4
Cantaloupe	267 g (1/2)	0.4
Blackberries	152 g (1 cup)	0.4
Banana	115 g (1 medium)	0.3
Apricots, fresh	105 g (3)	0.3
Dates, dried	80 g (10)	0.2
Pineapple, canned	164 g (1 cup)	0.2
Grapefruit juice, bottled	250 mL (1 cup)	0.2
Prunes, dried	40 g (5)	0.2
Raisins	76 g (1/2 cup)	0.2
Strawberries, fresh or frozen	157 g (1 cup)	0.2
Orange juice, frozen, diluted	250 mL (1 cup)	0.2
Blueberries	153 g (1 cup)	0.1
Grape juice, bottled	250 mL (1 cup)	0.1
Peach	87 g (1)	0.1
Orange	131 g (1)	0.1
Nectarine	136 g (1)	0.1
Watermelon, cubed	169 g (1 cup)	0.1
Cherries, fresh	109 g (1 cup)	0.1
Rhubarb, cooked, sweetened	127 g (1/2 cup)	0.1
Grapefruit	118 g (1/2)	0.1
Mango	207 g (1 medium)	0.1
Apple juice	250 mL (1 cup)	0.1
Plum, fresh	66 g (1)	0.1
Apple	138 g (1 medium)	0.1
Kiwi	76 g (1 large)	–

(–) Value not available in references consulted.

VEGETABLES	QUANTITY	ZINC (mg)
Green peas, cooked	169 g (1 cup)	2
Spinach, cooked	190 g (1 cup)	1.4
Collards, cooked	145 g (1 cup)	1.2
Beet greens, cooked	145 g (1 cup)	0.8
Summer squash, cooked	190 g (1 cup)	0.7
Potato, baked, with skin	206 g (1 medium)	0.6
Corn, frozen, cooked	173 g (1 cup)	0.6
Sweet potato, cooked	144 g (1 cup)	0.6
Broccoli, raw	151 g (1 spear)	0.6
Asparagus, cooked	120 g (8 spears)	0.6
Broccoli, cooked	164 g (1 cup)	0.5
Brussels sprouts, cooked	165 g (1 cup)	0.5
Winter squash, cooked	217 g (1 cup)	0.5
Turnip, cooked	165 g (1 cup)	0.5
Green beans, cooked	132 g (1 cup)	0.5
Beets, cooked	180 g (1 cup)	0.4

VEGETABLES	QUANTITY	ZINC (mg)
Okra, cooked	84 g (1/2 cup)	0.4
Tomatoes, cooked, canned	254 g (1 cup)	0.4
Parsnips, cooked	165 g (1 cup)	0.4
Mushrooms, cooked	41 g (1/2 cup)	0.4
Carrots, cooked	165 g (1 cup)	0.3
Mushrooms, raw	74 g (1 cup)	0.3
Spinach, raw	59 g (1 cup)	0.3
Kale, cooked	110 g (1 cup)	0.3
Cauliflower, raw	106 g (1 cup)	0.3
Zucchini, raw	190 g (1 cup)	0.2
Cauliflower, cooked	190 g (1 cup)	0.2
Dandelion greens, raw	60 g (1 cup)	0.2
Endive, raw	50 g (1 cup)	0.2
Lettuce, leaf, raw	59 g (1 cup)	0.2
Red cabbage, shredded, raw	74 g (1 cup)	0.1
Eggplant, cooked	101 g (1 cup)	0.1
Carrot, raw	72 g (1 medium)	0.1
Tomato, raw	123 g (1 medium)	0.1
Beet greens, raw	60 g (1 cup)	0.1
Green pepper, raw	73 g (1 medium)	0.1
Cabbage, shredded, raw	74 g (1 cup)	0.1
Leek, cooked	124 g (1 spear)	0.1
Swiss chard, raw	38 g (1 cup)	–
Swiss chard, cooked	185 g (1 cup)	–
Dandelion greens, cooked	105 g (1 cup)	–
Mustard greens, raw	60 g (1 cup)	–
Mustard greens, cooked	140 g (1 cup)	–

(–) Value not available in references consulted.

MEAT, FISH, POULTRY	QUANTITY	ZINC (mg)
Oysters, raw*	90 g (6 medium)	67
Pork liver, cooked	90 g (3 oz)	6.0
Beef, lean, cooked	90 g (3 oz)	5.2
Crab, canned	90 g (3 oz)	4.5
Beef liver, cooked	90 g (3 oz)	4
Chicken liver, cooked	90 g (3 oz)	3.9
Veal roast, cooked	90 g (3 oz)	3.7
Lamb chop, lean, cooked	90 g (3 oz)	3
Sardines, canned, with bones	90 g (3 oz)	2.7
Pork roast, cooked	90 g (3 oz)	2.6
Herring, canned	90 g (3 oz)	2.4
Ham, lean, cooked	90 g (3 oz)	2.3
Shrimp, canned	90 g (3 oz)	2.1
Lobster, canned	90 g (3 oz)	1.6
Chicken, without skin, cooked	90 g (3 oz)	0.9
Salmon, canned, with bones	90 g (3 oz)	0.8

MEAT, FISH, POULTRY	QUANTITY	ZINC (mg)
Tuna, canned	90 g (3 oz)	0.7
Egg, cooked	50 g (1)	0.5
Cod, broiled	90 g (3 oz)	0.4
Calves' liver, cooked	90 g (3 oz)	–
Scallops, cooked	91 g (7)	–
Clams, canned	90 g (3 oz)	–
Trout, broiled	90 g (3 oz)	–
Boston bluefish, broiled	90 g (3 oz)	–
Halibut, broiled	90 g (3 oz)	–
Sole, cooked	90 g (3 oz)	–
Haddock, raw	90 g (3 oz)	–

(–) Value not available in references consulted.
* *Best food investment.*

LEGUMES	QUANTITY	ZINC (mg)
Black-eyed peas, cooked	264 g (1 cup)	3
Chickpeas, cooked	211 g (1 cup)	2.7
Lentils, cooked	211 g (1 cup)	2
Red kidney beans, cooked	195 g (1 cup)	1.9
Lima beans, cooked	180 g (1 cup)	1.3
Lima beans, frozen, cooked	201 g (1 cup)	1
Pinto beans, cooked	95 g (1 cup)	0.9
Tofu	120 g (4 oz)	–
Soybeans, cooked	190 g (1 cup)	–
White kidney beans, cooked	137 g (1 cup)	–
Split peas, cooked	211 g (1 cup)	–
Black beans, cooked	200 g (1 cup)	–

(–) Value not available in references consulted.

MILK AND MILK PRODUCTS	QUANTITY	ZINC (mg)
Ricotta	130 g (1/2 cup)	1.4
Gruyère	30 g (1 oz)	1.2
Yogurt, plain	129 g (1/2 cup)	1.1
Gouda	30 g (1 oz)	1.1
Swiss cheese	30 g (1 oz)	1.1
Edam	30 g (1 oz)	1
Whole milk	250 mL (1 cup)	1
Buttermilk	250 mL (1 cup)	1
2% milk	250 mL (1 cup)	1
Skim milk	250 mL (1 cup)	1
Cheddar	30 g (1 oz)	0.9
Provolone	30 g (1 oz)	0.9
Colby	30 g (1 oz)	0.9
Feta	30 g (1 oz)	0.8
Mozzarella, partially skimmed	30 g (1 oz)	0.8
Blue	30 g (1 oz)	0.7

MILK AND MILK PRODUCTS	QUANTITY	ZINC (mg)
Brick	30 g (1 oz)	0.7
Mozzarella	30 g (1 oz)	0.7
Brie	30 g (1 oz)	0.7
Ice cream, vanilla	70 g (1/2 cup)	0.7
Camembert	30 g (1 oz)	0.7
Skim milk powder	8 g (2 tbsp)	0.6
Roquefort	30 g (1 oz)	0.6
Sliced cheese (processed)	30 g (1 oz)	0.5
Cottage cheese (2%)	120 g (1/2 cup)	0.5

NUTS AND SEEDS	QUANTITY	ZINC (mg)
Pecans	16	1.5
Cashews	14 large	1.3
Brazil nuts	4 large	0.9
Sunflower seeds, dried	18 g (2 tbsp)	0.8
Sesame seeds, whole, dried	9.5 g (1 tbsp)	0.7
Sesame butter, stone ground	14 g (1 tbsp)	0.7
Almonds	15	0.5
Peanut butter	16 g (1 tbsp)	0.5
Walnuts	5 halves	0.3
Hazelnuts (filberts)	10	0.3
Coconut, sweetened, dried	25 g (1/4 cup)	0.3
Pistachios	30	0.2

Table 2

BREADS AND CEREALS	QUANTITY	B_6 (mg)
Bran flakes*	40 g (3/4 cup)	0.6
Brown rice, cooked*	206 g (1 cup)	0.5
Pasta, whole-wheat, uncooked	100 g (3 1/2 oz)	0.4
Wheat germ	30 g (1/4 cup)	0.3
Bran cereal (All Bran)	35 g (1/2 cup)	0.27
Shreddies	43 g (3/4 cup)	0.25
Oat flakes, cooked	123 g (1/2 cup)	0.24
White rice, enriched, cooked	92 g (1 cup)	0.23
Raisin Bran	42 g (3/4 cup)	0.18
Pearl barley, cooked	105 g (1/2 cup)	0.1
Bran muffin	40 g (1 medium)	0.08
Shredded Wheat	25 g (1 biscuit)	0.06
Pumpernickel bread	32 g (1 slice)	0.05
Whole-wheat bread	28 g (1 slice)	0.04
Egg noodles, enriched, cooked	169 g (1 cup)	0.04
Macaroni, enriched, cooked	148 g (1 cup)	0.03
Wheat bran	4.2 g (1 tbsp)	0.03
Rye bread	25 g (1 slice)	0.02

BREADS AND CEREALS	QUANTITY	B₆ (mg)
White bread, enriched	24 g (1 slice)	0.01
Bagel	50 g (1)	–
Cream of Wheat, enriched, cooked	121 g (1/2 cup)	–
Red River cereal, cooked	125 g (1/2 cup)	–
Cream of Wheat, not enriched, cooked	121 g (1/2 cup)	–
Millet, dry	51 g (1/4 cup)	–

(–) Value not available in references consulted.
* *Best food investment*

FRUIT	QUANTITY	B₆ (mg)
Banana*	115 g (1 medium)	0.66
Prune juice, bottled	250 mL (1 cup)	0.59
Dates, dried	80 g (10)	0.42
Cantaloupe	267 g (1/2)	0.31
Avocado	173 g (1/2)	0.28
Mango	207 g (1 medium)	0.28
Watermelon, cubed	169 g (1 cup)	0.24
Figs, dried	95 g (5)	0.21
Pineapple, canned	164 g (1 cup)	0.19
Raisins	76 g (1/2 cup)	0.17
Grape juice, bottled	250 mL (1 cup)	0.17
Orange juice, frozen, diluted	250 mL (1 cup)	0.11
Prunes, dried	40 g (5)	0.11
Strawberries, fresh or frozen	157 g (1 cup)	0.09
Blackberries	152 g (1 cup)	0.08
Orange	131 g (1)	0.08
Apple juice	250 mL (1 cup)	0.08
Apple	138 g (1 medium)	0.06
Apricots, fresh	105 g (3)	0.06
Plum, fresh	66 g (1)	0.05
Blueberries	153 g (1 cup)	0.05
Grapefruit juice, bottled	250 mL (1 cup)	0.05
Grapefruit	118 g (1/2)	0.05
Cherries, fresh	109 g (1 cup)	0.05
Nectarine	136 g (1)	0.03
Rhubarb, cooked, sweetened	127 g (1/2 cup)	0.03
Peach	87 g (1)	0.01
Kiwi	76 g (1 large)	–

(–) Value not available in references consulted.
* *Best food investment.*

VEGETABLES	QUANTITY	B₆ (mg)
Mustard greens, frozen, cooked*	140 g (1 cup)	1.62
Potato, baked, with skin	206 g (1 medium)	0.70
Sweet potato, cooked	144 g (1 cup)	0.51

VEGETABLES	QUANTITY	B₆ (mg)
Brussels sprouts, cooked	165 g (1 cup)	0.45
Corn, frozen, cooked	173 g (1 cup)	0.36
Green peas, cooked	169 g (1 cup)	0.34
Spinach, cooked	190 g (1 cup)	0.28
Winter squash, cooked	217 g (1 cup)	0.27
Asparagus, cooked	120 g (8 spears)	0.25
Broccoli, cooked	164 g (1 cup)	0.24
Broccoli, raw	151 g (1 spear)	0.24
Tomatoes, cooked, canned	254 g (1 cup)	0.23
Cauliflower, raw	106 g (1 cup)	0.21
Beet greens, raw	60 g (1 cup)	0.20
Leek, cooked	124 g (1 spear)	0.20
Beet greens, cooked	145 g (1 cup)	0.19
Carrots, cooked	165 g (1 cup)	0.19
Summer squash, cooked	190 g (1 cup)	0.18
Kale, cooked	110 g (1 cup)	0.18
Cauliflower, cooked	190 g (1 cup)	0.16
Parsnips, cooked	165 g (1 cup)	0.15
Red cabbage, shredded, raw	74 g (1 cup)	0.15
Okra, cooked	84 g (1/2 cup)	0.15
Zucchini, raw	190 g (1 cup)	0.15
Dandelion greens, raw	60 g (1 cup)	0.14
Tomato, raw	123 g (1 medium)	0.14
Green pepper, raw	73 g (1 medium)	0.12
Spinach, raw	59 g (1 cup)	0.11
Turnip, cooked	165 g (1 cup)	0.11
Carrot, raw	72 g (1 medium)	0.10
Eggplant, cooked	101 g (1 cup)	0.09
Collards, cooked	145 g (1 cup)	0.08
Green beans, cooked	132 g (1 cup)	0.07
Mushrooms, raw	74 g (1 cup)	0.07
Cabbage, shredded, raw	74 g (1 cup)	0.07
Beets, cooked	180 g (1 cup)	0.05
Mushrooms, cooked	41 g (1/2 cup)	0.04
Lettuce, leaf, raw	59 g (1 cup)	0.03
Endive, raw	50 g (1 cup)	0.01
Swiss chard, raw	38 g (1 cup)	–
Swiss chard, cooked	185 g (1 cup)	–
Dandelion greens, cooked	105 g (1 cup)	–
Mustard greens, raw	60 g (1 cup)	–

(–) Value not available in references consulted.
* *Best food investment.*

MEAT, FISH, POULTRY	QUANTITY	B₆ (mg)
Beef liver, cooked	90 g (3 oz)	0.77
Salmon, raw	90 g (3 oz)	0.63
Calves' liver	90 g (3 oz)	0.60

MEAT, FISH, POULTRY	QUANTITY	B₆ (mg)
Chicken, without skin, cooked	90 g (3 oz)	0.58
Chicken liver, cooked	90 g (3 oz)	0.56
Pork liver, cooked	90 g (3 oz)	0.51
Salmon, canned, with bones	90 g (3 oz)	0.42
Beef, lean, cooked	90 g (3 oz)	0.39
Halibut, broiled	90 g (3 oz)	0.39
Pork roast, cooked	90 g (3 oz)	0.38
Lamb chop, lean, cooked	90 g (3 oz)	0.32
Ham, lean, cooked	90 g (3 oz)	0.30
Veal roast, cooked	90 g (3 oz)	0.30
Crab, canned	90 g (3 oz)	0.27
Tuna, canned	90 g (3 oz)	0.24
Cod, broiled	90 g (3 oz)	0.20
Sardines, canned, with bones	90 g (3 oz)	0.16
Haddock, raw	90 g (3 oz)	0.16
Herring, canned	90 g (3 oz)	0.14
Boston bluefish, broiled	90 g (3 oz)	0.11
Shrimp, canned	90 g (3 oz)	0.09
Clams, canned	90 g (3 oz)	0.07
Egg, cooked	50 g (1)	0.05
Oysters, raw	90 g (6 medium)	0.05
Scallops, cooked	91 g (7)	–
Lobster, canned	90 g (3 oz)	–
Trout, broiled	90 g (3 oz)	–
Sole, cooked	90 g (3 oz)	–

(–) Value not available in references consulted.

LEGUMES	QUANTITY	B₆ (mg)
Soybeans, cooked	190 g (1 cup)	0.85
Lentils, cooked	211 g (1 cup)	0.57
Chickpeas, cooked	211 g (1 cup)	0.54
Pinto beans, cooked	95 g (1 cup)	0.50
White kidney beans, cooked	137 g (1 cup)	0.39
Lima beans, cooked	180 g (1 cup)	0.32
Red kidney beans, cooked	195 g (1 cup)	0.30
Lima beans, frozen, cooked	201 g (1 cup)	0.24
Black-eyed peas, cooked	264 g (1 cup)	0.18
Split peas, cooked	211 g (1 cup)	0.09
Tofu	120 g (4 oz)	–
Black beans, cooked	200 g (1 cup)	–

(–) Value not available in references consulted.

NUTS AND SEEDS	QUANTITY	B₆ (mg)
Hazelnuts (filberts)	10	0.17
Sunflower seeds, dried	18 g (2 tbsp)	0.14
Cashews	14 large	0.07
Sesame seeds, whole, dried	9.5 g (1 tbsp)	0.07

NUTS AND SEEDS	QUANTITY	B₆ (mg)
Peanut butter	16 g (1 tbsp)	0.06
Walnuts	5 halves	0.05
Pecans	16	0.05
Coconut, sweetened, dried	25 g (1/4 cup)	0.05
Brazil nuts	4 large	0.05
Pistachios	30	0.04
Sesame butter, stone ground	14 g (1 tbsp)	0.02
Almonds	15	0.02

MILK AND MILK PRODUCTS	QUANTITY	B₆ (mg)
Feta	30 g (1 oz)	0.13
2% milk	250 mL (1 cup)	0.10
Whole milk	250 mL (1 cup)	0.10
Skim milk	250 mL (1 cup)	0.10
Cottage cheese (2%)	120 g (1/2 cup)	0.08
Buttermilk	250 mL (1 cup)	0.08
Brie	30 g (1 oz)	0.07
Camembert	30 g (1 oz)	0.06
Yogurt, plain	129 g (1/2 cup)	0.06
Skim milk powder	8 g (2 tbsp)	0.05
Ricotta	130 g (1/2 cup)	0.05
Blue	30 g (1 oz)	0.05
Roquefort	30 g (1 oz)	0.04
Ice cream, vanilla	70 g (1/2 cup)	0.03
Swiss cheese	30 g (1 oz)	0.02
Colby	30 g (1 oz)	0.02
Gouda	30 g (1 oz)	0.02
Gruyère	30 g (1 oz)	0.02
Cheddar	30 g (1 oz)	0.02
Edam	30 g (1 oz)	0.02
Provolone	30 g (1 oz)	0.02
Mozzarella, partially skimmed	30 g (1 oz)	0.02
Sliced cheese (processed)	30 g (1 oz)	0.02
Brick	30 g (1 oz)	0.02
Mozzarella	30 g (1 oz)	0.01

Table 3

Nutrients (Additive)	Recommended Allowances for Females Age 10 to 75 Plus[1][2]	Low Risk Dose	Best Form*	Toxic Dose	Special Concerns for Each Nutrient
VITAMIN A	4,000 IU (800 RE) per day	25,000 IU	• Beta-carotene • Vitamin A acetate or palmitate	• Toxicity well-documented at doses of 50,000 IU (10,000 RE) or more.	• Mineral oil inhibits absorption of vitamin A • Needs increase during pregnancy by 500-2,000 IU per day and during lactation by 2,000-3,000 IU per day. • During pregnancy, doses of 15,000 IU and more may cause birth defects • Use of vitamin A and its derivatives in the treatment of acne requires the supervision of a physician. One's food habits should be modified as well. • Beta-carotene is not toxic, unlike retinol, which can be at high doses.
VITAMIN D	100-400 IU (2.5-10μg) per day	400-800 IU (10-20 μg)	D₂ or D₃ (added to milk)	• Toxicity well-documented at doses of 25,000 IU and more. • Even lower doses have been known to cause problems.	• Needs increase by 100-200 IU per day during pregnancy and lactation. • Strict vegetarians should be careful to get enough vitamin D. • Dark-skinned women need 3 hours of exposure to the sun compared to light-skinned women, who need 30 minutes of exposure, to get a full day's supply of vitamin D. • It is not advisable to take more than 10 ml (2 tsp) per day of cod liver oil, a natural source of vitamin D.

* If this information is not available on the label, ask your pharmacist.

Table 3

Nutrients (Additive)	Recommended Allowances for Females Age 10 to 75 Plus[1-2]	Low Risk Dose	Best Form*	Toxic Dose	Special Concerns for Each Nutrient
VITAMIN E	5-8 mg per day	300-400 mg	• dl-alpha tocopheryl acetate • d-alpha tocopheryl acetate	• Isolated reports of toxic effects at doses of 800 mg or more.	• Needs increase during pregnancy by 2 mg per day and during lactation by 3 mg per day. • The association between hot flashes and vitamin E has yet to be demonstrated. • A vitamin E supplement may decrease breast tenderness during the premenstrual period.
THIAMIN[3] (B₁)	1-1.1 mg per day	Appears non-toxic	• Thiamin mononitrate • Thiamin hydrochloride	• No known toxic effects reported	• Needs increase during pregnancy by 0.3-0.4 mg per day and during lactation by 0.5 mg per day. • It is difficult to meet needs during pregnancy and lactation. (Brewer's yeast, pork, soybeans, white kidney beans, and liver are among the richest sources of thiamin.)
RIBOFLAVIN[3] (B₂)	1.2 mg per day	Appears non-toxic	Riboflavin	No known toxic effects reported	• Vigorous exercise may double requirements. • Needs increase during pregnancy by 0.3 mg per day and during lactation by 0.3-0.5 mg per day. • Strict vegetarians, not drinking milk, may have difficulty meeting their needs.

NIACIN[3] (B$_3$)	13-15 mg per day	100-300 mg	Niacinamide	• Short-term effects (eg. rashes) may occur at doses of 100 mg. • Long-term effects occur at doses of 100-300 mg plus.	• Needs increase during pregnancy by 2.5 mg per day and during lactation by 5-9 mg per day.
PYRIDOXINE[3] (B$_6$)	1.5-2 mg per day	50-100 mg	• Pyridoxine hydrochloride • Pyridoxal-5[1] phosphate	• Reversible nerve damage at doses of 2,000 mg or more.	• Needs increase during pregnancy by 0.6 mg and during lactation by 0.5 mg per day. • According to a preliminary report, 200 mg or more may interfere with breast feeding. • Supplements of 25-50 mg have been shown to retrieve some symptoms of premenstrual tension. • Women who take oral contraceptives may have increased needs for B$_6$. • The relationship between B$_6$ and nausea in pregnancy remains controversial.
VITAMIN C (ascorbic acid)	40-60 mg per day	500-1000 mg	• Sodium ascorbate • Calcium ascorbate • Ascorbic acid	• Reports of diarrhea and kidney stones at doses of 100 mg or more.	• Chewable tablets may erode tooth enamel. • 75 mg of vitamin C at each meal, whether in the form of food or as a supplement, aids in the absorption of iron. • Smokers have increased needs for vitamin C. • Needs increase during pregnancy by 20 mg per day and during lactation by 30-40 mg per day.

Table 3

Nutrients (Additive)	Recommended Allowances for Females Age 10 to 75 Plus[1-2]	Low Risk Dose	Best Form*	Toxic Dose	Special Concerns for Each Nutrient
CALCIUM	800 mg (adult women) 700-1200 mg (adolescents) per day	1800-2500 mg	• Calcium carbonate	• Doses of 2,500 mg or more per day may cause problems.	• Needs increase during pregnancy by 400-500 mg per day and during lactation by 400-500 mg per day. • If there is a problem with kidney stones, drink plenty of water. • Take supplements with a meal or snack.
MAGNESIUM	160-300 mg per day	1,000 mg	• Magnesium oxide	• 1,700 mg or more, in the form of magnesium containing antacids, or laxatives, have been associated with adverse effects.	• Needs increase during pregnancy by 25-150 mg per day and during lactation by 80-150 mg per day. • Women with kidney problems should not take more than 600 mg per day.
IRON	10-18 mg per day	25-30 mg	• Ferrous sulphate • Ferrous fumarate	• Doses of 18 mg or more can cause constipation and stomach upset.	• Supplements of iron are recommended during pregnancy. • Needs increase during pregnancy and lactation (see page 000).

ZINC	7-15 mg per day	15-25 mg	• Zinc sulphate	• Joint pain may occur at doses of 100 mg or more. • Reports of adverse effects at doses of 50 mg or more. • High doses reportedly reduce HDL cholesterol (so-called "good" cholesterol)	• Needs increase during pregnancy by 2-5 mg per day and during lactation by 6-10 mg per day.
SELENIUM	50-200 µg per day (suggested as adequate and safe for adults)	350-500 µg	• Sodium selenate	• Toxicity well-documented at doses of 2,400-3,000 µg	• Selenium appears to have a role in the prevention of cancer. • Best food sources are organ meats, seafood, muscle meats, whole grains (amount depends on the selenium content of the soil).
CHROMIUM	50-200 µg per day (suggested as adequate and safe for adults)	200 µg	• Chromium chloride	• Not known, possibly due to lack of use.	• Chromium enhances the action of insulin. • Best food sources include Brewer's yeast, liver, beef, poultry, whole grains, bran, wheat germ. • Refined foods are poor sources of chromium.

Nutrients (Additive)	Recommended Allowances for Females Age 10 to 75 Plus[1-2]	Low Risk Dose	Best Form*	Toxic Dose	Special Concerns for Each Nutrient
VITAMIN B$_{12}$ (cobalamine)	1-3 µg per day	Appears non-toxic	Cyano-cobalamine	• None known	• Needs increase during pregnancy by 1 µg per day and during lactation by 0.5-1 µg per day. • Strict vegetarians, who consume no dairy products, must take a supplement during pregnancy and lactation.
FOLACIN	145-400 µg per day	400 µg	• Folic acid	• May increase zinc excretion at doses of 400 µg or more.	• Needs increase during pregnancy by 305-400 µg per day and during lactation by 100-120 µg per day. • The use of supplemental folic acid and iron is recommended during pregnancy. • Oral contraceptive use may induce folacin deficiency in some women.
PANTO-THENIC ACID	4-10 mg (considered adequate for adults)	Appears non-toxic	• Calcium pantothenate • D-panthenol	• Reports of adverse effects at doses of 200-20,000 mg	(—)

1. *Recommended Nutrient Intakes for Canadians*. Health and Welfare Canada, Ottawa, 1983. *Recommended Dietary Allowances*, 9th Edition. Natural Research Council, Washington, D.C., 1980.
2. Requirements for non-pregnant, non-lactating, healthy females.
3. Requirements for B vitamins for Canada are based on the 1975 recommendations.
(—) No information available.

Table 4

"Natural" Supplements	Available Forms	What We Know (Action and Nutritional Properties)
LECITHIN (Scientific name: phosphatidylcholine)	• Commercial product prepared with soya lecithin, gelatin, glycerine and purified water. • May contain only 20-30% lecithin	• Lecithin is found naturally in soybeans, liver, eggs, peanuts, wheat germ. • It is used as an emulsifier in a number of food products. • At high doses it can increase HDL (the "good" cholesterol) and decrease triglycerides and cholesterol. • High intakes may produce gastrointestinal distress, sweating and a loss of appetite.
ALFALFA	• Leaves of alfalfa are dried, ground, and sold in powder form or as pills.	• Rich in vitamins E, K, D, B vitamins and calcium. • Certain components of alfalfa can interfere with the utilization of vitamin E and destroy red blood cells. • No proof demonstrated of its effectiveness in treating diabetes.
WHEAT GERM OIL	• Sold in bottle or in capsule form.	• Contains polyunsaturated fatty acids. • Is an excellent source of vitamin E: 15 ml (1 tbsp) contains 28 IU.
BLACKSTRAP MOLASSES	• By-product of the refining of white sugar. • Syrup left after the 3rd extraction.	• Very pronounced taste. • Good source of iron and calcium. • Has a laxative effect. • 15 ml (1 tbsp) contains 3.4 mg of iron and 144 mg of calcium.
WHEAT BRAN	• The outside covering of the whole grain. • Sold in bulk. • Sold in the form of a supplement found in fiber-rich biscuits sold in the pharmacy.	• Rich in non-soluble fibers. • Contains some minerals and vitamins found in the grain. • Has a laxative effect—avoid taking more than 30 ml (2 tbsp) to begin with. • Promotes intestinal regularity. • "Oat bran," rich in "soluble" fibers appears to have a cholesterol lowering effect.

"Natural" Supplements	Available Forms	What We Know (Action and Nutritional Properties)
COD LIVER OIL	• Sold in bottle or in capsule form. • Sometimes mint flavored.	• Excellent source of vitamin D and A. • Contains omega-3 type fatty acids (page 000). • Can be toxic when taken in large quantities, because of its contents of vitamin A and D which are toxic at high doses. • 5 ml (1 tbsp) contains 44 calories, 28 mg of cholesterol, 350 IU of vitamin D, and 3,500 IU of vitamin A. • Do not take more than 10 ml (2 tsp) per day.
EVENING PRIMROSE OIL	• "Gamma-linolenic acid"—a polyunsaturated oil. • Sold in capsules.	• Contains "essential fatty acids" as does corn oil and sunflower seed oil. • Can be absorbed without the help of the enzyme "delta-6-desaturase." • Appears to relieve chronic skin problems (acne, eczema) • Helps to reduce premenstrual tension in some women.
DOLOMITE	• Mixture of approximately equal parts calcium carbonate and magnesium carbonate. • Sold in tablet form.	• Is used as a supplement of calcium and magnesium. • Does not contain vitamin D.
BONE MEAL	• Powder obtained from the finely ground bones of animals. • Sold in powder or tablet form.	• Is used as a supplement of calcium. • Does not contain vitamin D. • May contain unsafe residues of arsenic and lead.
YEAST • BREWER'S • TORULA • ENGEVITA	• Brewer's yeast has a very pronounced taste. • Sold in powder or in tablet form. • The nutritive value of 2-8 tablets is much less than that of 15 ml (1 tbsp) of powdered yeast. • Torula yeast is grown on pulp and engevita yeast on molasses (milder tasting).	• Particularly rich in B vitamins, iron, folic acid, chromium, selenium, potassium, phosphorus. • Contains vitamin B_{12} if grown on a medium to which B_{12} has been added. • Rich in nucleic acids. • Can constitute a protein supplement between meals: 30 ml (2 tbsp) contains 5 g of protein.

GARLIC OIL	• Sold in tablet form with or without parsley, as a syrup, in odorless capsules, or as essential oil.	• Has a diuretic and vasodilator effect. • Some research has shown an effect on fat in the blood (a decrease in cholesterol and triglycerides). • Consumption of large doses produces gas, garlicky breath, and body odor.
GINSENG	• Powder derived from the root of the "panax ginseng" plant. • Sold in capsules, powder, paste, tea, whole root, and tablet forms.	• May cause an increase in blood pressure in some individuals. • May cause breast pain and vaginal bleeding in some post-menopausal women. • Some products are devoid of the "active" ingredient. • At doses as low as 3 g, side-effects have been reported (hypertension, neurological symptoms).
SEAWEED (Alga) "Agar-Agar" "Kelp" "Spirulina" "Hijiki noir" "Nori" "Dulse"	• Sold in powder or tablet form or as dried filaments. • Agar-Agar is sold in strips or as flakes and is used to replace gelatin.	• Kelp is rich in iodine as are the other seaweeds. • Seaweed is generally rich in minerals. • Spirulina contains proteins and nucleic acids. • Most of the vitamin B_{12} in spirulina is not biologically active and can even interfere with the active form. (Herbert, V., "A new look at vitamin B_{12}" in issues in *Vegetarian Dietetics*, II, 1988.) • Seaweed incorporated into the cooking water of legumes, seems to decrease the problem of flatulence associated with the latter.

References:
Tyler, V.E., *The New Honest Herbal*, George Stikley Co., Philadelphia, 1982.
Worthington-Roberts, B. et al, "Facts or Fads? A pharmacist's guide to controversial nutrition products", *American Pharmacy*, n 523, 1983, pages 31–42.
Lambert-Lagacé, L., "Les suppléments naturels", presentation to the Congrès de la Cité de la Santé, May 24, 1985.

Bibliography

On Women's Dietary Deficiencies

Butte, N. et al., "Effect of maternal diet and body composition on lactational performance," in *American Journal of Clinical Nutrition*, 39, 1984, pp. 296-306.

Clarck, A.J. et al., "Folacin status in adolescent females," in *American Journal of Clinical Nutrition*, 46, 1987, pp. 302-306.

Crandall, C., "Do men and women differ in emotional and ego involvement with food," in *Journal of Nutrition Education*, 19, 1987, pp. 229-236.

Crosby, F.J., *Spouse, Parent, Worker, on Gender and Multiple Roles*, Yale University Press, New Haven, 1987.

Driskell, J.A. et al., "Longitudinal assessment of vitamin B_6 status in southern adolescent girls," in *Journal of the American Dietetic Association*, 87, 1987, pp. 307-310.

Dupin, H., and J.P. Mareschi, "Habitudes alimentaires, modes de vie, apports nutritionnels: implications technologiques," in *Réalisations 1984*, La Fondation française pour la nutrition, 1985, pp. 33-44.

Endres, G. et al., "Older pregnant women and adolescents; nutrtion data after enrollment in WIC," in *Journal of the American Dietetic Association*, 87, 1987, pp. 1011-1016.

Enns, C.W., "Comparison of nutrient intakes by male vs female heads of households," in *Journal of the American Dietetic Association*, 87, 1987, pp. 1551-1553.

Franklin, N., "Starved self-esteem," in *Medical Self Care*, 29, 1985, p. 41.

Gibson, R.S. et al., "Dietary fiber and selected nutrient intakes of some Canadian children, adolescents and women," in *Journal of the Canadian Dietetic Association*, 48, 1987, pp. 82-87.

Havens, C., "Premenstrual syndrome. Tactics for intervention," in *Post-graduate Medicine*, 77, 1985, pp. 32-37.

Hercberg, S. et al., "Statut en fer au cours de la grossesse: étude mul-ticentrique dans la région parisienne," in *Groupes à risque de carence en fer dans les pays industrialisés*, Dupin and Hercberg ed., INSERM symposium, 113, 1983, pp. 69-88.

Hercberg, S. et al., "Le statut en fer du sujet âgé," in *L'alimentation des personnes âgées*, Maison de la chimie, Paris, 1985, pp. 127-138.

Hoint, F., "Enquête sur l'alimentation spontanée de jeunes adultes parisiens," in *Médecine et nutrition*, 23, 1987, pp. 91-94.

Jones, D.Y. et al., "Premenstrual syndrome: a review of possible dietary influences," in *Journal of the Canadian Dietetic Association*, 44, 1983, pp. 194-200.

Kurinij, N. et al., "Dietary supplement and food intake in women of childbearing age," in *Journal of the American Dietetic Association*, 86, 1986, pp. 1536-1540.

Lopez, L.M. et al., "Food stamps and iron status of the US elderly poor," in *Journal of the American Dietetic Association*, 87, 1987, pp. 598-603.

Mareschi, J.P. et al., "The well balanced diet and, at risk, micro-nutrients. A forecasting nutritional index," in *International Journal of Vitamin and Nutrient Research*, 57, 1987, pp. 79-85.

Morgen, K.T. et al., "Magnesium and calcium dietary intakes of the US population," in *Journal of the American College of Nutrition*, 4, 1985, pp. 195-206.

Murphy, S.D., and D. Calloway, "Nutrient intakes of women in NHANES 11, emphasizing trace minerals fiber and phytate," in *Journal of the American Dietetic Association*, 86, 1986, pp. 1366-1372.

O'Connor, D. et al., "Dietary calcium and phosphorus intakes of a sample of Canadian post-menopausal women consuming self-selected diets," in *Journal of the Canadian Dietetic Association*, 46, 1985, pp. 45-49.

Pennington, J.A. et al., "Mineral content of food and total diets; the selected minerals in foods surveys 1982 to 1984," in *Journal of the American Dietetic Association*, 86, 1986, pp. 876-891.

Posner, B.E. et al., "Dietary characteristics and nutrient intake in an urban homebound population," in *Journal of the American Dietetic Association*, 87, 1987, pp. 452-456.

Rouaud, C. et al., "Consommation alimentaire d'étudiantes de la région parisienne: étude particulière du magnésium," in *Médecine et Nutrition*, 22, 1986, pp. 295-301.

Seoane, N. et al., "Selected indices of iron status in adolescents," in *Journal of the Canadian Dietetic Association*, 46, 1985, pp. 298-303.

Sevenhuysen, G.P. et al., "Nutrient intakes of women and school children in northern Manitoba native communities," in *Journal of the Canadian Dietetic Association*, 48, 1987, pp. 89-93.

Sims, L., "Dietary Status of lactating women. 1. Nutrient intake from food and from supplements," in *Journal of the American Dietetic Association*, 73, 1978, pp. 139-146.

USDA, "Nationwide food consumption survey, continuing survey of food intakes by individuals. Women 19-50 years and their children 1-5 years, 1 day," in *NFCS, CSFII, Report no. 85-1*, 1985.

Viglietti, G.C., and J.D. Skinner, "Estimation of iron bioavailability in adolescents' meals and snacks," in *Journal of the American Dietetic Association*, 87, 1987, pp. 903-908.

Zuckerman, D.M. et al., "Prevalence of bulimia among college students," in *American Journal of Public Health*, 76, 1986, pp. 1135-1137.

On Fear of Gaining Weight

American Diabetes Association, "Position Statement. Use of non-caloric sweeteners," in *Diabetes Care*, 10, 1987, p. 526.

Bjorntorp, P., "Adipose tissue in obesity (Willendorf lecture)," in *Recent Advances in Obesity: IV*, John Libbey Company Limited, London-Paris, 1985, pp. 163-170.

Blundell, J.E. et al., "Paradoxical effects of an intense sweetener (aspartame) on appetite," in *The Lancet 1* (8489), 1986, pp. 1092-1093.

Bradstock, M.K. et al., "Evaluation of reactions to food additives: the aspartame experience," in *American Journal of Clinical Nutrition*, 43, 1986, pp. 464-469.

Butte, N. et al., "Effect of maternal diet and body composition on lactational performance," in *American Journal of Clinical Nutrition*, 39, 1984, pp. 296-306.

CDA, *A Healthy Weight in 1988*, The Canadian Dietetic Association, Toronto, 1987.

Counihan, C.M., "What does it mean to be fat, thin and female in the United States: a review essay," in *Food and Foodways*, 1, 1985, pp. 77-94.

Dalvit, S.P., "The effect of menstrual cycle on patterns of food intake," in *American Journal of Clinical Nutrition*, 34, 1981, pp. 1811-1815.

De Boer, J.O. et al., "Adaptation of energy metabolism of overweight women to low-energy intake, studied with whole-body calorimeters," in *American Journal of Clinical Nutrition*, 44, 1986, pp. 585-595.

Edwards, L.E. et al., "Pregnancy in the underweight woman. Course, outcome and growth patterns of the infant,"in *American Journal of Obstetrics and Gynecology*, 135, 1979, pp. 297-302.

Evers, C., "Dietary intake and symptoms of anorexia nervosa in female university dancers," in *Journal of the American Dietetic Association*, 87, 1987, pp. 66-68.

Franklin, N., "Starved self esteem," in *Medical Self Care*, 29, 1985, p. 41.

Garrow, J.S., and J. Webster, "Quetelet's index (W/H2) as a measure of fatness," in *International Journal of Obesity*, 9, 1985, pp. 147-153.

Grunewald, K.K., "Weight control in young college women—who are the dieters," in *Journal of the American Dietetic Association*, 85, 1985, pp. 1445-1450.

Higgins, A. et al., "Nutritional status and the outcome of pregnancy," in *Journal of the American Dietetic Association*, 37, 1976, p. 17-35.

Kirkley, B.G., "Bulimia: clinical characteristics, development and etiology," in *Journal of the American Dietetic Association*, 86, 1986, p. 468.

Lapidus. L. et al., "Dietary habits in relation to incidence of cardiovascular disease and death in women: a 12-year follow-up of participants in the population study of women in Gothenburg, Sweden," in *American Journal of Clinical Nutrition*, 44, 1986, pp. 444-448.

Liebman, B.F., "Is dieting a losing game?" in *Nutrition Action Healthletter*, 14, 1987, pp. 10-11.

Nelson, M.E., "Diet and bone status in amenorrheic runners," in *American Journal of Clinical Nutrition*, 43, 1986, pp. 910-916.

Palin, D., and D. Rankine, "Nutrition durant la grossesse—lignes directrices nationales: un aperçu," in *Journal of the Canadian Dietetic Association*, 48, 1987, pp. 211-213.

Palmer, J.L. et al., "Development of an assessment form: attitude toward weight gain during pregnancy," in *Journal of the American Dietetic Association*, 85, 1985, pp. 946-949.

Spodnik, M.J. et al., "Fluid retention and weight reduction in perimenopausal women," in *Journal of the American Dietetic Association*, 85, 1985, pp. 971-972.

Sours, H. et al., "Sudden death associated with very low-calorie weight reduction regimens," in *American Journal of Clinical Nutrition*, 34, 1981, pp. 453-461.

Stellman, S.D. et al., "Artificial sweetener use and one year weight change among women," in *Preventive Medicine*, 15, 1986, pp. 195-202.

Taffel, S.M. et al., "Advice about weight gain during pregnancy and actual weight gain," in *American Journal of Public Health*, 76, 1986, pp. 1396-1399.

Tomelleri, R. et al., "Menstrual cycle and food cravings in young college women," in *Journal of the American Dietetic Association*, 87, 1987, pp. 311-315.

Toufexis, A., "Dieting: the losing game," in *Time*, Jan. 20, 1986, pp. 52-60.

Toufexis, A., "Have your cake—and eat it too," in *Time*, Feb. 8, 1988, pp. 50-52.

Van Itallie, T.B. et al., "Some hazards of obesity and its treatment," in *Recent Advances in Obesity Research: IV*, John Libbey Company Limited, London-Paris, 1985, pp. 1-20.

Webb, P., "24-hour energy expenditure and the menstrual cycle," in *American Journal of Clinical Nutrition*, 44, 1986, pp. 614-619.

Worthington-Roberts, B., "Preconceptional and prenatal nutrition: Part 1—energy, protein and related issues," in *Journal of the Canadian Dietetic Association*, 46, 1986, p. 169.

On Lack of Time

Clarkson, Gordon, and Gordon Woods, *Tomorrow's Customers*, Toronto, 1987.

Conseil consultatif canadien sur la situation de la femme, *Participation et intégration: Les femmes, le travail, et l'argent*, C.P. 1541, succursale, Ottawa, KIP 5R5.

Cyr, R. et al., *Les repas congelés*, Département de santé communautaire de Sherbrooke, Sherbrooke, 1986.

Ladies Home Journal, "What's happening to mealtime?" New York, 1979, 90 pages.

Nevraumont, U., "Where Canadians buy their food and when," in *Food Market Commentary*, 9, 1987, pp. 49-53.

On Eating Out

Baum, D., "Dietary treatment of transmeridian dyschronesia," in *Nutrition Today*, Nov.-Dec. 1983, p. 29.

Flowers-Willett, L. et al., "Energy content of selected salad bar and hot serving line meals," in *Journal of the American Dietetic Association*, 85, 1985, pp. 1630-1633.

Green, E.M. and H. Appledorf, "Proximate and mineral content of restaurant steak meals," in *Journal of the American Dietetic Association*, 82, 1983, pp. 142-147.

Lambert-Lagacé, L. "Boîte à lunch pour femme active," in *Châtelaine*, September 1985, pp. 84-89.

Lambert-Lagacé, L., and S. Dubois, "Déjeuner d'affaires: repas hypocalorique," in *Le médecin du Québec*, April 1980, pp. 109-118.

Moore, L., "Eating smart when you travel," in *Working woman*, April 1986, pp. 164-168.

Perrault, D., "Les habitudes alimentaires," in *L'hospitalité*, Nov.-Dec. 1987, pp. 18-20.

Regan, C., "Promoting nutrition in commercial food service establishments: a realistic approach," in *Journal of the American Dietetic Association*, 87, 1987, pp. 486-488.

Ries, C.P. et al., "Impact of commercial eating on nutrient adequacy," in *Journal of the American Dietetic Association*, 85, 1985, pp. 463-468.

Sherbanowski, J., "Women travelers," in *Food service and Hospitality*, March 1987, pp. 20-24.

On Living Alone

Davies, L., *Easy Cooking for One or Two*, Penguin Books, 1981.

On Unconventional Diets

CPDQ, *Mise au point concernant les combinaisons alimentaires*, Corporation professionnelle des diététistes du Québec, Montréal, 1987.

Crisafi, D., "Candida, l'autre maladie du siècle," Forma, Montréal, 1987.

Crook, W.G., *The Yeast Connection*, Vintage Books, New York, 1986.

Diamond, H. and M., *Fit for Life*, Warner Books, New York, 1985.

Hill, J., "Food fads and fears," in *Cooks*, January 1988, p. 3.

Kousmine, C., *Soyez bien dans votre assiette jusqu'à 80 ans ou plus*, Primeur Sand, Paris, 1985.

Lecong, A., "Nutritional status and dietary intake of a selected sample of young adult vegetarians," in *Journal of the Canadian Dietetic Association*, 47, 1986, pp. 101-106.

Martin-Bordeleau, L., *Les combinaisons alimentaires*, Éd. Lazer, Montréal, 1986.

Mérien, D., *Compatibilités alimentaires*, Éd. Nature et vie, Lorient, 1986.

Oshawa, G. *Zen Macrobiotics*, Oshawa Foundation Inc., Los Angeles, 1965.

Shelton, H.M., *Les combinaisons alimentaires et votre santé*, Éd. La nouvelle hygiène, Paris, 1968.

On Fat, Iron, Calcium and Magnesium

Astier-Dumas, M. et al., "Densité nutritionnelle en magnésium. À propos de quelques produits prêts à consommer," in *Médecine et Nutrition*, 20, 1984, pp. 397-399.

Brady, H. et al., "Magnesium. The forgotten ration," in *Irish Medical Journal*, 80, 1987, pp. 250-253.

CDA, "Alimentation et prévention du cancer. Prise de position de l'Association canadienne des diététistes," in *Revue de l'Association canadienne des diététistes*, 48, 1987, pp. 146-148.

Chan, G.M. et al., "Effects of increasing dietary calcium intake upon the calcium and bone mineral status of lactating adolescent and adult women," in *American Journal of Clinical Nutrition*, 46, 1987, pp. 319-323.

Committee on Diet, Nutrition and Cancer, National Research Council. *Diet Nutrition and Cancer*, National Academy Press, Washington, D.C., 1982.

Dallman, P., "Iron deficiency and the immune response," in *American Journal of Clinical Nutrition*, 46, 1987, pp. 329-334.

Dawson-Hughes, B. et al., "Dietary calcium intake and bone loss from the spine in healthy post-menopausal women," in *American Journal of Clinical Nutrition*, 46, 1987, pp. 685-687.

Draper, H., "Le calcium alimentaire et la prévention de l'ostéoporose post-ménopausique," in *Étude no. 1*, Institut national de nutrition, Ottawa, May 1987.

Drueke, T. et al., "Minéraux en alimentation humaine," in *Cahiers de nutrition et de diététique*, 21, 1986, pp. 341-354.

Durlach, J., "Le magnésium: métabolisme, besoins et indices diététiques et thérapeutiques," in *Nouvelles archives hospitalières*, 42, 1970, pp. 31-40.

Dyerberg, J., "Linolenate-derived polyunsaturated fatty acids and prevention of atherosclerosis," in *Nutrition Reviews*, 44, 1986, pp. 125-133.

Farley, M.A., "Adult dietary characteristics affecting iron intake. A comparison based on iron density," in *Journal of the American Dietetic Association*, 87, 1987, pp. 184-189.

Grundy, S.M., "Monounsaturated fatty acids (n-3, n-6)," in *American Journal of Clinical Nutrition*, 45, 1987, pp. 1168-1175.

Hallberg, L., "Iron," in *Present Knowledge in Nutrition*, fifth edition, The Nutrition Foundation Inc., Washington, D.C., 1984, pp. 459-477.

Herbert, V., "Recommended dietary intakes RDI for iron in humans," in *American Journal of Clinical Nutrition*, 45, 1987, 679-686.

Kelsay, J.L., "Effects of fiber, phytic acid and oxalic acid in the diet on mineral bioavailability," in *American Journal of Gastroenterology*, 82, 1987, pp. 983-985.

Kremer, J.M. et al., "Fish oil fatty acid supplementation in active rheumatoid arthritis," in *Annals of Internal Medicine*, 106, 1987, pp. 497-503.

Lamisse, F., "Fibres alimentaires. Place des fibres céréalières," in *Cahiers de nutrition et de diététique*, 22, 1987, pp. 397-406.

Léger, C., "Les acides gras essentiels ont-ils une fonction structuro-modulatrice membranaire spécifique," in *Cahiers de nutrition et de diététique*, 22, 1987, pp. 105-115.

Marier, J.R., "Magnesium content of the food supply," in *Magnesium*, 5, 1986, pp. 1-8.

Mensick, R.P., "Effect of Monounsaturated fatty acids and prevention of atherosclerosis," in *The Lancet 1* (8525), 1987, pp. 121-125.

Meunier, P.J., "Les troubles osseux du troisième âge: possibilités de prévention," in *L'alimentation des personnes âgées*, Département de santé de CIDIL, Paris, 1985, pp. 53-62.

Meyers, L.D. et al., "Prevalence of anemia and iron deficiency anemia in black and white women in the United States estimated by two methods," in *American Journal of Public Health*, 73, 1987, pp. 1042-1049.

Morris, E.R., "An overview of current information on bioavailability of dietary iron to humans," in *Federation Proceedings*, 42, 1983, pp. 1716-1720.

Nestel, P.J., "Polyunsaturated fatty acids (n-3, n-6)," in *American Journal of Clinical Nutrition*, 45, 1987, pp. 1168-1175.

O'Neil-Cutting, M.A. et al., "The effect of antacids on the absorption of simultaneously ingested iron," in *Journal of the American Medical Association*, 225, 1986, pp. 1468-1470.

Piclet, G., "Le poisson aliment," in *Cahiers de nutrition et de diététique*, 22, 1987, pp. 317-335.

Salle, B., "Alimentation et développement du squelette," in *Réalisations 1984*, La Fondation française pour la nutrition, Paris, 1985, pp. 5-8.

Seelig, M.S., "Magnesium requirements in human nutrition," in *Contemporary Nutrition*, January 7, 1982.

Sempos, C.T., "A two-year dietary survey of middle aged women—repeated dietary records as a measure of usual intake," in *Journal of the American Dietetic Association*, 84, 1984, pp. 1003-1008.

Smith, T.M. et al., "Absorption of calcium from milk and yogourt," in *American Journal of Clinical Nutrition*, 42, 1985, pp. 1197-1200.

Société canadienne du cancer, *Le cancer et le régime alimentaire*, Canada, October 1985.

Whang, R., "Magnesium deficiency causes and clinical implications," in *Drugs*, 28, suppl. 1, 1984, pp. 143-150.

Sources Consulted for Preparation of Nutrition Tables

Brault-Dubuc M. and Caron-Lahaie L., *Valeur nutritive des aliments*, Université de Montréal, 1987.

Health and Welfare Canada, *Nutrient value of some common foods* Revised edition, Canada, 1987.

Randoin, L. et al., *Tables de composition des aliments*, Édition Jacques Lanore, Paris, 1985.

Robertson L. et al., *Laurel's Kitchen. A Handbook for Vegetarian Cookery and Nutrition*, Nilgiri Press, 1976.

USDA Human Nutrition Information Service, *Agriculture Handbook Number 8. Composition of Foods.*
—Dairy and Egg Products 8-1, 1976 revision.
—Spices and Herbs 8-2, 1977 revision.
—Poultry Products 8-5, 1979 revision.
—Breakfast Cereals 8-8, 1982 revision.
—Fruit and Fruit Juices, 8-9 1982 revision.
—Pork Products 8-10, 1983 revision.
—Vegetables and Vegetable Products 8-11, 1984 revision.
—Nut and Seed Products, 1984 revision.

Recipe Index

Breakfast Suggestions

Healthy Blender Breakfast, 52   Hot Cereal Supreme, 83

Desserts and Dessert Sauces

Instant Dessert, 56   Strawberry Coulis, 56

Main Courses: Lunch or Dinner

Chinese-Style Liver, 111   Light Quiche, 54
Chicken with Julienned   Magic Soufflé, 82
   Vegetables, 58–59   Shepherd's Pie with Lentils, 151
Herb-Steamed Fish, 57–58   Spinach and Tofu Quiche, 153

Sauces and Dressings

Ginger Sauce for White Fish, 55   Seafood Sauce, 55
Light Sauce for Poultry, 56   Summer Sauce, 55
Pesto, 51   Vinaigrette, 53

Snacks

Meal in a Glass, 83   Vitamin-Rich Snacks, 53
Muffin à la Mode, 81

Soups

Broccoli Soup, 150   Minute Soup, 52
Minute Minestrone, 82

Vegetables and Salads

Health Salad, 53   Vegetables al dente, 54

Index

Acne, 6, *tables*, 163, 170
Adolescence. *See* Puberty and
   the teen years.
Ailments, women's, 5, 16–17
Alcohol,
   and calcium absorption, 123
   and fatigue, 68, 70, 71
   and magnesium requirements,
   134
   consumption by women, 11,
   16, 18.
   See also Wine.
Alfalfa, *table*, 169
American College of Allergists
   and Immunologists, 91
American College of
   Obstetricians and
   Gynecologists, 29
American Pharmacy, cited, 171
Anemia, 4, 9, 17, 106
Anorexia nervosa, 17
   effects, 28, 33
Anti-candida diet, 90–91
   effects, 90–91
   explained, 90
   not recommended, 90
   regarded as experimental, 91
Anti-jet-lag formula, 70–71
Arthritis, 6, 41, 105
Aspartame. *See* Sugar
   substitutes.

"Best investment." *See* under
   Food.
Birth defects,
   and nutrition, 30–31, 88
   from excess vitamin A, *table*,
   163
Birth weight,
   and mother's weight, 30–31

Blackburn, Dr., 38
Blackstrap molasses, 96, 109,
   table, 169
Blood donation,
   and iron loss, 107–108
Blood pressure,
   and nutrition, 85
   lower in vegetarians, 87
Body Mass Index (BMI), 24–26
   exceptions to BMI
   interpretation, 26
   table, 25
Bone meal, *table*, 170
Bronwell, Dr., 33
Bulimia, 2, 4, 17
   effects, 28
Butter. *See* Dairy Products.

Calcium,
   absorption and estrogen, 23,
   123
   absorption, facilitated,
   122–123; inhibited, 123–124
   adequate, 88, 95–88, 118–129,
   table, 120; 121
   and iron absorption, 110
   and magnesium, 133–134
   and menopause, 9, 119
   and post-menopausal women,
   1, 119, 121, 122
   and vitamin D, 122–123
   as additive nutrient, *table*, 166
   content of foods, *tables*,
   124–129
   cooking tips, 124
   deficiencies, 9, 33, 61, 62, 86,
   90, 97, 118–120
   supplements, 121
Calories,
   and metabolism, 34–36

and nutrition, 11–12
consumption, 11–12, 84–85, 101, 143
effects of shortage, 86
excess in restaurant meals, 61–62
requirements during pregnancy, 31, 101
requirements when nursing, 31, 101
Canada
Department of Health and Welfare, 16, 24; as source for *tables*, 113, 168
Canadian Cancer Society, 99
Canadian Diabetic Association, 99
Cancer, 6
and fat consumption, 99, 105
and nutrition, 85
Candida albicans, 90
Cardiovascular problems,
and role of magnesium, 130
less in vegetarians, 87
vulnerability, 104
Châtelaine, 2
Cheese. *See* Dairy Products.
Cholesterol,
and weight gain, 23
decrease in vegetarianism, 87
excess, 6, 98
reducing levels, 103–105, *table*, 171
Chromium, *table*, 167
Cobalamine. *See* Vitamin B$_{12}$
Cod liver oil, 105, *tables*, 163, 170
Coffee
after meal, 65
and calcium loss, 123
Columbia University, 33
Constipation, 4
less in vegetarians, 87
Cooking
and men, 13–14

and women, 13–15, 17, 18
delegation, 49, 80
fast but healthy, 47–48; *recipes*, 51–19, 81–83, 74–75
for freezer, 50–51
improved methods, 36, 57
participation in, 50–51
to save time, 66–67, 75
Corbeil, Diane, 5
Crook, Dr. William, 90
Cyclamates. *See* Sugar substitutes.

Dairy products,
and balanced nutrition, 36–37, 39, 47, 64–71, 75–79
calcium content, *table*, 128
fat content, *tables*, 100, 101, 102; 104
in "improved menu plan," 143–144
iron content, *table*, 116–117
lacto-vegetarian meals, 70, 71, 87
magnesium content, *table*, 138
vitamin B$_6$ content, *table*, 162–163
zinc content, *table*, 157–158
Davies, W.H., 40
Davis, Adele, 84
Deschêne, Mme, 81
Diabetes, 6, 23
Diet books, 1, 22
Diets,
and calcium loss, 33
anti-candida, 90–91
and undernourishment, 4, 33, 85–91, 153
as a trap, 14, 15
as an obsession, 22
evaluating nutritional balance, 91–92
food combination, 85–87
macrobiotic, 89

radical, 1, 6, 21, 33, 84–92,
    143, 153
vegetarian, 9, 87–88
Digestive problems, 4, 86, 90
Diuretics,
    abuse of, 28
Dolomite, *table*, 170
Dougherty, Cynthia, 5
Dubois, Sheila, 5

Eating,
    enjoyment, 14–15, 41
    psychology of, 12–13, 41,
        72–74, 95–105, 153
Eating disorders. *See* Anorexia
    nervosa; Bulimia.
Entertaining,
    grandchildren, 81
    simplified, 74–75
Enzymes, 86, 106, 108
Estrogen,
    and calcium absorption, 23
    and the menstrual cycle, 32
Evening primrose oil, *table*, 170
Exercise,
    excessive, 29
    healthy, 36

Fat,
    content of foods, *tables*,
        99–101, 102
    decreasing consumption,
        36–37, 39, 63, 87, 95–105
    excess, and magnesium
        absorption, 134
    excess consumption, 9, 84–85,
        98–99
    in balanced diet, 98–105
    in fast food, 46, 61
    in "improved menu plan,"
        144
    in restaurant meals, 62
    omega 3 fatty acids, 104–105
    omega 6 fatty acids, 105

Fat substitutes, 37
Fat tissue and women, 1, 23
Fatigue,
    and alcohol, 68, 70, 71
    and iron deficiency, 106
    and women, 1
    in *Candida albicans*, 90
Fiber, dietary,
    biscuits, 68
    deficient consumption, 9–10,
        46, 61
    increasing consumption, 36,
        62, 87
    and calcium absorption, 124
    and iron absorption, 110
Fish and seafood,
    and balanced nutrition, 36,
        39, 47–48, 63–71, 75–79
    calcium content, *table*, 127
    fat content, *tables*, 100, 101
    in "improved menu plan,"
        144
    iron content, *table*, 115–116
    magnesium content, *table*, 137
    omega 3 fatty acids in,
        104–105
    vitamin B$_6$ content, *table*,
        160–161
    zinc content, *table*, 156–157
Fit for Life, 86
Folacin, *table*, 168
Food,
    and contemporary women,
        14–15, 40–51
    and women's traditional role,
        12–13
    as compensation, 2–3, 12, 72
    "best investment," for
        calcium, *tables*, 124–129; for
        iron, 96, *tables*, 113–117; for
        low fat, 98–105; for
        magnesium, 132–133, *tables*,
        134–139; for vitamin B$_6$,
        tables, 154, 156; for zinc,

tables, 158, 159
dietetic, 10, 37–39
enjoyment, 14–15, 41
fast-, 14, 46, 60
freezing fresh, 50–51
in restaurants, 60–65
instant, 10
"light", 37–39, 47
loss of confidence in, 84–85
natural, 85
quality, 10–12, 27–29, 35–37,
  39, 47–48, 61–62, 84–85
quantity, 10–12, 27–29, 36, 63,
  81–83, 84–85
seasonal, 50–51
shopping for, 49–50, 75–79
simplifying preparation,
  51–52, 74–75, *recipes*, 51–59,
  81–83
Food combination diet, 84, 85
effects of, 86–87
explained, 86–87
not recommended, 86–87
Food processors, 51, 79
Food technology, 10–11
Fruit,
  and balanced nutrition, 36,
    39, 47–48, 63–71, 75–79
  fat content, *table*, 101
  freezing fresh, 50
  in "improved menu plan,"
    143
  iron content, *table*, 114
  magnesium content, *table*, 136
  vitamin B₆ content, *table*, 159
  zinc content, *table*, 155

Gallstones,
  incidence in women vs men,
    17
Garlic oil, *table*, 171
Gentle dietetics, 34–37, 95
Ginseng, *table*, 171
Grain products, 48

and balanced nutrition, 36,
  48, 62–71, 75–79
calcium content, *table*, 125
fat content, *tables*, 100, 101
in "improved menu plan,"
  144, *table*, 144–145
iron content, *table*, 113–114
magnesium content, *table*, 135
vitamin B₆ content,
  table, 158–159
zinc content, *table*, 154
Grandchildren,
  tip for entertaining, 81

Harvard Medical School, 38
Health, good,
  definition, 3–4
  related to nutrition, 4
Heaney and Recker, 123
Heart disease,
  and magnesium, 130
  and nutrition, 29, 33, 85
  in family history, 98
Herbs,
  as seasoning, 75, 78
  calcium content, *table*, 129
  drying, 51
  iron content, *table*, 117
  magnesium content, *table*, 139
Hypertension, 6, 23
Hypoglycemia, 6

Illness,
  and nutrition, 5, 6
"Improved menu plan,"
  See under Menus.
Inactivity,
  and calcium loss, 119, 124
  and fat consumption, 101
  and magnesium deficiency,
    131, 134
Infertility, 29
Iron,
  absorption, facilitated, 110,

tables, 112–113; inhibited,
  65, 86, 110
adequate, 88, 95–98, 106–117,
  table, 108
as additive nutrient, *table*, 166
content of foods, *tables*,
  113–117
cooking tips and *recipe*,
  108–112
deficiencies, 9, 11, 62, 90, 97,
  106–108
women's vs men's needs, 11,
  107

Jet lag,
  to prevent, 70–71

Kidney disease, *table*, 166

Lactose intolerance, 119–120
Laxatives,
  abuse of, 28
Lecithin, *table*, 169
Leftovers, nutritious, 66–67
Legumes, pulses,
  and balanced nutrition, 47,
    64, 66, 67, 77, 79
  calcium content, *table*,
    127–128
  fat content, *tables*, 100, 101
  in "improved menu plan,"
    144
  iron content, table, 116
  magnesium content, *table*, 138
  vitamin B₆ content, *table*, 161
  zinc content, *table*, 157
Lifestyles,
  and eating out, 60–65
  and time demands, 6, 18,
    40–59
  and travel, 68–71
  contemporary, 1, 15–16, 17,
    18, 41–46, 72–81
  healthy, 37, 46–59

Living or being alone,
  and older women, 17, 72, 81
  and women's nutrition, 6, 21,
    44–45, 72–83, 153
  psychology of, 72–74
Lunch, packed,
  tips for nutritious, 65–67

Macrobiotics, 84
  effects of, 89
  explained, 89
  not recommended, 89
  yin and *yang*, 89
Magnesium,
  absorption, facilitated, 133;
    inhibited, 133–134
  adequate, 87, 95–98, 131–139,
    table, 132
  and calcium, 130, 133–134
  and processed food, 130–131
  as additive nutrient, *table*, 166
  content of foods, *tables*,
    134–139
  cooking tips, 134
  deficiencies, 9, 97, 130–132
  functions, 131
Margarine. *See* under Oils.
Mayo Clinic, 17
Meat,
  and balanced nutrition, 36,
    47, 62–71, 76–79
  calcium content, *table*, 127
  fat content, *tables*, 100, 101
  in "improved menu plan,"
    144
  iron content, *table*, 115–116
  magnesium content, *table*, 137
  vitamin B₆ content, *table*,
    160–161
  zinc content, *table*, 156–157
Menopause and after
  and calcium requirements, 1,
    9, 119, 121, 122
  and cholesterol levels, 98

and discomfort, 17
and hormonal swings, 11, 32
and iron requirements, 107
and nutritional needs, 31–33,
    107–108, 119–121, 131, 145
and weight, 31–33
Menstruation,
    and discomfort, 16
    and food cravings, 31–32
    and hormonal swings, 11, 32
    and iron loss, 11, 106–107
    and iron requirements,
        107–108
    disruption of, 29
Menus,
    for easy entertaining, 74–75
    "improved menu plan," 109,
        122, 141–150, *recipes*,
        150–152
    in anti-jet-lag formula, 71
    restaurant, and nutrition, 6,
        60–65
Metabolism,
    and calorie consumption,
        34–36
    at menopause, 32
    during menstruation, 32
    women's, 10
Metropolitan Tables, 23–24
Microwave, 48, 50, 51, 79–80,
    note, 79–80
Milk. *See* Dairy products.
Montreal Diet Dispensary, 30
Multiple sclerosis, 6

"Natural" Supplement Tables,
    169–171
New England Journal of Medicine,
    27
The New Honest Herbal, cited,
    171
Niacin, *table*, 165
Nutrient (Additive) Tables,
    163–168

Nutrition, women's
    and good health, 4, 5, 35–37,
        39, 85, 145, 153
    and heart disease, 29
    and "light" foods, 37–39
    and restaurant menus, 6, 21,
        60–65
    and solitude, 6, 21, 72–74
    available literature, 1
    awareness, 84–85
    balanced, 47–48, 60–71,
        72–83, 88, 91–92, 95–105,
        106–117, 118–129, 130–139,
        145, 146–153
    deficiencies, 9–18, 27–34, 46,
        72, 84–91, 95–105, 106–108,
        118–120, 130–132, 153
    differing theories of, 85
    knowledge about, 5, 84–85
Nutritional guidance,
    for dieting, 91–92
    individual, 6
    in vegetarianism, 88
Nutritional needs,
    and the "improved menu
        plan," 146–153
    at menopause and after, 31–33,
        107–108, 119–121, 131, 145
    calcium requirements,
        118–124
    difficulties in meeting, 1, 2,
        9–18, 21, 40–46, 84, 153
    fat in diet, 98–105
    iron requirements, 107–110
    of men and women, 1, 6,
        11–12, 61–62, 63, 76, 107, 153
    of nursing mothers, 31, 76,
        88, 101, 107–108, 119–120,
        131, 132, 145, *tables*,
        163–168
    of pregnant women, 1, 9,
        29–31, 76, 88, 101, 107–108,
        119–120, 131, 132, 145,
        tables, 163–168

Nutritional strategy,
  as basis of book, 6, 153
  as gentle dietetics, 95–105
  for living alone, 72–83
  for packed lunches, 65–67
  for restaurant meals, 62–65
  for saving time, 46–59
  to avoid jet lag, 70–71
  when traveling, 68–69
Nuts and seeds,
  and balanced nutrition, 66–71
  calcium content, *table*,
    128–129
  fat content, *table*, 101
  iron content, *table*, 117
  magnesium content, *table*,
    138–139
  unsalted, as snack, 36, 48
  vitamin B$_6$ content, *table*,
    161–162
  zinc content, *table*, 158

Oils, cooking
  cold-pressed
    polyunsaturated, 103 (and
    note)
  linseed, *note* 105
  margarine, types, 104
  mono-unsaturated, 104
  partly hydrogenated
    vegetable, 104
  polyunsaturated, 103–104
  virgin (first-press) olive, 104
Oshawa, George, 89
Osteoporosis,
  and calcium deficiency,
    118–119
  and weight, 23, 32
  incidence in women vs men,
    17

Pantothenic acid, *table*, 168
Physical activity,
  and calcium absorption, 122

and contemporary women,
    10
  and magnesium
    requirements, 132
  and teenage women, 27
  women vs men, 16
Poletti, Rosette, 4
Poliquin, Suzette, 5
Potassium,
  increasing consumption, 87
Poultry,
  and balanced nutrition, 36,
    47–48, 63, 64, 66–69, 71,
    75, 78
  calcium content, *table*, 127
  fat content, *tables*, 100, 101
  in "improved menu plan,"
    144
  iron content, *table*, 115–116
  magnesium content, *table*,
    137
  vitamin B$_6$ content, *table*,
    160–161
  zinc content, *table*, 156–157
Poverty,
  and women, 17, 18
Pregnancy,
  and additive nutrients, *tables*,
    163–168
  and calcium requirements,
    119, 122
  and iron requirements,
    107–108
  and nutritional requirements,
    2, 9, 29–31, 88, 101, 145
  and weight gain, 23, 26,
    29–31
Progesterone,
  and the menstrual cycle, 32
Protein,
  absorption of, 86
  and calcium absorption, 123
  and magnesium absorption,
    134

deficiencies, 9, 86
high-content prepared foods, 47
high-content quick-to-prepare foods, 47
Ptyalin. *See* Enzymes.
Puberty and the teen years,
and calcium requirements, 118–119, *table*, 120
and fat requirements, 101
and "improved menu plan," 145
and iron requirements, 107, *table*, 108
and magnesium requirements, 131, *table*, 132
and normal growth, 27
and nutrition deficiencies, 9, 42
and weight, 26–27
Pulses. *See* Legumes, pulses.
Pyridoxine. *See* Vitamin B₆

Quetelet Index. *See* Body Mass Index (BMI).

Restaurants,
and women, 21, 80, 153
"croissant," 61
fast-food, 46, 61
menus and nutrition, 6, 60–65
salad bars, 61
Riboflavin,
adequate, 88
as additive nutrient, *table*, 164

Saccharine. *See* Sugar substitutes.
Salt,
decreasing consumption, 36, 60

in fast food, 46
Seafood. *See* Fish and seafood.
Seaweed, *table*, 171
Selenium, *table*, 167
Self-esteem,
and good health, 3, 27, 35
and women's vs men's roles, 14
loss of, 28
Shellfish. *See* Fish and seafood.
Shelton, Herbert, 85–87
Shopping,
delegation of, 49
for one, 75–79
grocery, 49
participation in, 50
Smoking,
and adolescent women, 16
and vitamin C, *table*, 165
and women, 16, 18
incidence of, 16
Snacks,
nutritious, 36, 47–48, 69
Soft drinks,
consumption, 10–11, 38, 84
Solitude. *See* Living or being alone.
Spices,
calcium content, *table*, 129
iron content, *table*, 117
magnesium content, *table*, 139
Sports,
and calcium absorption, 122
and health, 27
and iron requirements, 108
and magnesium requirements, 132
Strokes, 105
Sugar,
decreasing consumption, 36, 39
in fast food, 46
Sugar substitutes, 37–39

and pregnant women, 38
and sensitivity to
phenylalamine, 38
and the U.S. Food and Drug
Administration, 38
and weight loss, 38
not recommended, 38
Sun, exposure to. *See* under
Vitamin D.
"Superwomen," 15
Surveys,
lifestyle, 16
National Natality (NNS), 30
nutritional, 9
women's weight, 22
women's work schedules,
40–41
Sweet tooth, 2, 84

Tea,
bancha, 89
black or green and iron
absorption, 65, 110
herbal, after meals, 65
Teenagers. *See* Puberty and the
teen years.
Thiamin, *table*, 164
Thinness,
as obsession, 4, 6, 14, 17–18,
21–39, 95
Thyroid gland,
and metabolism, 32
Time shortage,
and lifestyle, 18, 21
as obstacle to nutrition,
40–46
case histories, 41–46
recipes to overcome, 51–59
redefined, 6
Triglycerides, 23, 105, *table*, 171
Trudel, Nicole, 5

University of Montreal, 5
University of Pennsylvania, 33

U.S. Food and Drug
Administration, 38
U.S. National Center for Health
Statistics, 30
U.S. National Research
Council, 99; as source for
table, 168

Vacuum-packed meals, 80
Van Itallie, Dr., 33
Vegetables,
and balanced nutrition, 36,
48, 62–71, 75, 79
calcium content, *table*,
126–127
fat content, *table*, 101
freezing fresh, 50–51
in "improved menu plan,"
143
iron content, *table*, 114–115
magnesium content, *table*,
136–137
raw, 36, 48
vitamin B₆ content, *table*,
159–160
zinc content, *table*, 155–156
Vegetarian Dietetics, cited, 171
Vegetarianism, 9, 87–88
advantages and
disadvantages, 87–88
balanced nutrition in, 88,
107, 119, 131, 145, *tables*,
163, 164, 168
lacto-ovo-vegetarians, 87
lacto-vegetarian meals, 70, 71
motives for, 87
semi-vegetarians, 87
strict vegetarians or vegans,
87–88
when not recommended, 88
Vitamin A,
as additive nutrient, *table*, 163
deficiencies, 61
Vitamin B₁. *See* Thiamin.

Vitamin B₃. *See* Niacin.
Vitamin B₆
   adequate, 96–98
   as additive nutrient, *table*, 165
   content of foods, *tables*,
     158–162
   deficiencies, 9, 62, 90, 97
Vitamin B₁₂
   adequate, 88
   as additive nutrient, *table*, 168
   deficiencies, 86, 90
Vitamin C,
   absorption, 86
   as additive nutrient, *table*, 165
   deficiencies, 61
   and iron absorption, 110,
     tables, 112–113
Vitamin D,
   adequate, 88
   and calcium, 122–123
   and exposure to the sun, 122,
     table, 163
   and magnesium, 133
   as additive nutrient, *table*, 163
   deficiencies, 86, 89
Vitamin E, *table*, 164

Weight,
   and nursing mothers, 23, 29
   and osteoporosis, 23, 32

and teenage women, 26–27
as obsession, 4, 6, 14, 15,
   17–18, 21–39
during menopause, 23, 29–33
during pregnancy, 23, 29–31
healthy, 24–26, *table*, 25
Weight-loss clinics, 17, 22
Wheat bran, *table*, 169
Wheat germ oil, *table*, 169
Wine, 11, 62, 74
   and iron absorption, 110
Women,
   and poverty, 17, 18
   and travel, 68–71
   and work, 15–16, 40–41
   as single parents, 17, 18

Yeast,
   as "natural" supplement,
     tables, 164, 170
   as snack, 69
Yin and *yang*, 89
Yogurt. *See* Dairy products.

Zinc,
   adequate, 96–98
   as additive nutrient, *table*, 167
   content of foods, *tables*,
     154–158
   deficiencies, 86, 97